Secret Practices
of the
Sufi Freemasons

Secret Practices
of the
Sufi Freemasons

The Islamic Teachings
at the Heart of Alchemy

Baron Rudolf von Sebottendorff

Translation, Introduction, and Commentary by
Stephen E. Flowers, Ph.D.

Inner Traditions
Rochester, Vermont • Toronto, Canada

Inner Traditions
One Park Street
Rochester, Vermont 05767
www.InnerTraditions.com

Originally published in German in 1924 under the title *Die Praxis der alten türkischen Freimauerei: Der Schlüssel zum Verständnis der Alchemie* by Theosophisches Verlagshaus.

Library of Congress Cataloging-in-Publication Data

Sebottendorff, Rudolf, Freiherr von, 1875–1945.
 [Praxis der alten türkischen Freimaurerei. English]
 Secret practices of the Sufi freemasons : the Islamic teachings at the heart of alchemy / Baron Rudolf von Sebottendorff ; translation, introduction, and commentary by Stephen E. Flowers.
 p. cm.
 "Originally published in German in 1924 under the title Die Praxis der alten türkischen Freimauerei: Der Schlüssel zum Verständnis der Alchemie by Theosophisches Verlagshaus."
 Includes bibliographical references and index.
 ISBN 978-1-59477-468-3 (pbk.) — ISBN 978-1-62055-001-4 (e-book)
 1. Freemasonry—Symbolism. 2. Freemasonry—Religious aspects—Islam. 3. Alchemy—Religious aspects—Islam. 4. Sufism. I. Flowers, Stephen E., 1953– II. Title.
 HS425.S3913 2013
 366ʹ.10882974—dc23

                                                                          2012020452

Printed and bound in the United States

10 9 8 7 6 5 4

Text design by Jack Nichols and layout by Priscilla Baker
This book was typeset in Garamond Premier Pro with Arbitrary, Agenda, and KaraBenNemsi used as display typefaces

Contents

The Practice of Ancient Turkish Freemasonry

THE KEY TO THE UNDERSTANDING OF ALCHEMY

A Presentation of the Ritual, Doctrine, and Signs of Recognition among the Oriental Freemasons

By Baron Rudolf von Sebottendorff

Introduction

You have before you a very strange book. It is a book of secret Sufi exercises based on a particular sect's teachings about certain sounds, gestures, and the so-called abbreviated letters found at the beginnings of certain chapters of the Qur'an. These exercises are reputed to be able to perfect the spirit of the individual. Furthermore, this particular book was written by a German expatriate and Turkish citizen, who is reputed by some to be the mastermind behind the formation of a political order that eventually became Hitler's Nazis. You have been warned that you are embarking on a strange adventure.

The text of the 1924 book titled *Die Praxis der alten türkischen Freimauerei* (The Practice of Ancient Turkish Freemasonry) is in itself unusual. Part of its content is well organized, clear, and concise; while other features of it are mixed with elements of a confusing and chaotic nature. The manual could have been even shorter. It really consists simply of a description and schedule of exercises to be conducted regularly over a period of many months. No concrete knowledge is imparted as to what these exercises will actually do for the individual—but it is clearly implied that the reward will be great and that all sorts of knowledge and wisdom will be imparted directly to the practitioner.

This book is intended to be nothing more than a translation of Sebottendorff's 1924 text with some explanatory information about the author, his ideas, and the general spiritual world that gave rise to the exercises. It is not an attempt to add anything new or different to the text, which stands on its own.

I am not a Muslim or a teacher of Sufism. I am just a humble scholar. No insult, slight, or disrespect is ever intended toward Muhammad, the Qur'an, or Islam. On the contrary, it is hoped that this book will open the eyes of a few more people to the great spiritual contributions of Islam to the mysterious world we all share in common.

STEPHEN E. FLOWERS
WOODHARROW

1

The Life of
Rudolf von Sebottendorff

Rudolf von Sebottendorff was a man of mystery. Much remains unknown about his life and his death. He is shrouded in legend and surrounded by misinformation. The true nature and motive of his life and work remain in question. That much of this obscurity was of his own manufacture is one thing that seems certain. The answers to these questions about the author of *Secret Practices of the Sufi Freemasons* may or may not be relevant to the understanding of the book you have before you. It may be that he simply acted as a conduit for these Sufi techniques to make their way into the West. This is at least part of what he seems to want to imply to the reader. Or it may be that his work in Germany after World War I—work that most people today would deem sinister— was a fundamental part of something intimately connected to the contents of *The Secret Practices of the Sufi Freemasons*. It seems most likely that the former is the truer of the two possibilities. The exercises were learned by Sebottendorff as part of his work with the Bektashi Order of dervishes in Istanbul. These and similar practices of Muslim orders, sects, and brotherhoods were seen by him to be essential in the age-old sense of solidarity and dedication to purpose inherent in these orders. These were qualities he wanted to re-instill in the German people (as he mentions in the text). Therefore, it is possible that the contents of the manual are not tainted with Sebottendorff's German nationalism; rather he simply wished to utilize the Sufi teachings in an attempt to regenerate German solidarity and dedication to purpose in the dismal time between the wars. In any event, the fascination this book has held for people over the years has stemmed more from the identity of its author than from the contents of the exercises. In this volume I wish to reorient attention to the substance of the Sufi practices, and away from the personality of the author. However, the fascinating and important story of the mysterious author's life cannot go unmentioned.

The first mystery of Baron Rudolf von Sebottendorff's life lies in the fact that he was not born a baron, nor was his name Sebottendorff. He obtained the name and title later in life. He was born Adam Alfred Rudolf Glauer in Hoyerswerda, near Dresden, on November 9, 1875. His father was a locomotive driver and veteran of the Prussian army, who fought in the Austro-Prussian campaign (1866) and the Franco-Prussian War (1871). Rudolf's father died in 1893 leaving enough money for his son to finish his formal education.

Glauer began training as a mechanical engineer, but never finished his studies. Instead he lived a life of adventure in exotic locales and on the high seas until 1900. In Australia, after attempting to prospect for gold, he received a letter of introduction from a Parsi (Zoroastrian) to a wealthy Turkish landowner, Hussain Pasha. He managed an estate at Bursa for this landowner, who was a practitioner of Sufism. He was also introduced there to the Termudi family. The patriarch of this Jewish family, originally from Greece, was a student of the Kabbalah and Rosicrucianism. Glauer was initiated into a Freemasonic lodge of which the Termudis were members. He remained in Turkey, learned Turkish, and studied occultism until 1902. Then he returned to Germany, but around 1908 some legal misadventures in Germany caused him to return to Turkey.

The next two years were pivotal for the adventurer. In 1910 he founded a mystical lodge in Constantinople—which is a *tariqat* of the Bektashi Order of Sufis. The next year he is legally adopted by the German expatriate Heinrich von Sebottendorff and also becomes a legal citizen of Turkey. This adoption was later repeated twice more by other Sebottendorff family members, all of which indicates just how important the acquisition of the noble title was to him.

During the Balkan War (1912–1913) he was on duty with the Red Crescent, the Islamic version of the Red Cross. He was actually wounded in battle and for a time a POW. After this he returned once more to Europe and lived in Berlin and Austria.

It was in the midst of the First World War (1914–1918) that Sebottendorff joined the Germanen Order (GO), at first by correspondence only. In September of 1916 he personally visited Hermann Pohl, who was the head of the order in Berlin. Subsequently Sebottendorff was elected master of the Bavarian province of the order and became the publisher of the GO publications.

The true nature and scope of the Germanen Order remains shadowy. Ostensibly it was formed as a sort of mystical lodge within the more politically oriented *Reichshammerbund* (Imperial Hammer League). The mastermind behind these groups was the notorious anti-Semite Theodor Fritsch (1852–1933).[1] Fritsch was instrumental in the invention of a biologically based anti-Semitism to appeal to those who had become disenchanted with the mass appeal of the age-old religion-based anti-Semitism, with its origins in the medieval church. The GO was essentially a pseudo-Masonic order with ritual based on Wagnerian imagery.[2]

As 1918 was drawing to a close, the fortunes of war and politics had turned against the Germans. The Great War was being lost and in Munich left-wing revolutionaries were clamoring for political power, inspired by recent success in the Russian Revolution (1917). The name *Thule-Gesellschaft* (Thule Society) was adopted by the Germanen Order as a cover identity.* The society met weekly in rented rooms at the Hotel Vierjahreszeiten (Four Seasons) in Munich. But it began to take on a life and identity of its own under Sebottendorff's leadership. Occult topics were the subject of lectures given by the baron—this in the midst of open revolution in the streets of Munich.

Sebottendorff only led the Thule Society from April 1918 to July 1919. During this time he formed a militia to fight the Communists, was instrumental in the formation of the German Workers' Party, and acquired a newspaper, the *Münchner Beobachter* (Munich Observer). In April of 1919, Communists seized power in Bavaria. In this process they took seven members of the Thule Society hostage and subsequently executed them. This atrocity became a rallying point for the right-wing militias. The militias were eventually successful in turning back the left-wing revolution. The German Workers'

---

*The word *Thule* comes from the Greek explorer and geographer Pythias, who made a journey to the far northern regions of the world around 310 BCE. He gave the name *Thule* to the land in the northernmost region.

Party was soon thereafter reformed by charismatic leader Adolf Hitler into the National Socialist German Workers' Party (*National-Sozialistische Deutsche Arbeiter Partei—NSDAP*), called *Nazis* by their detractors. The newspaper was bought by that party and transformed into its mouthpiece—*Der völkische Beobachter* (The Nationalist Observer).

Obviously all of these facts point to Sebottendorff's deep involvement with what was to become the Nazi movement in post-WWI Germany. It also seems clear that Sebottendorff and others were guided and financed in their efforts. What is less certain is how much these men were engineers of these efforts and how much they were mere pawns.

The chronology of Sebottendorff's life shows that he was mostly involved in personal adventure and spiritual or magical pursuits—with a short, active career (1916–1919) as a political operative under the cover of occult organizations. After he left Munich in July of 1919, he returned to esoteric studies and writing. For fifteen years he continued in his esoteric pursuits and it is during this period that he wrote and published most of his major works, including *The Secret Practices of the Sufi Freemasons.*

Astoundingly, Sebottendorff returned to Germany after Hitler took power in 1933, tried to revive the Thule Society, and published a book, which seemed to try to take credit for getting the National Socialist movement started from within the Thule Society. The book was entitled *Bevor Hitler kam* (Before Hitler Came). The Nazis were not pleased. Sebottendorff was arrested twice; the book was banned, confiscated, and destroyed in 1934. He returned to Turkey. This whole adventure appeared to be simply an attempt to cash in on the success of the Nazis, an attempt that failed. Or perhaps it did not fail entirely. The post-1934 life of the baron is quite mysterious. He was put on the payroll of the German Intelligence Service in Istanbul. His handler was Herbert Rittlinge. Turkey had been an ally of Germany in WWI, but in WWII it remained neutral until the very end of the war, when it joined the Allied side. In 1944 the German embassy was closed in Turkey, and Sebottendorff was given his severance pay of one year's support. On May 8, 1945, Germany surrendered unconditionally. Sebottendorff died that same day.

Some controversy surrounds the death of Sebottendorff. The usual story is that he committed suicide by jumping off a bridge in Istanbul right after hearing of Germany's surrender. If this is true it was probably more out of the desperation of a septuagenarian man with no prospects for the future than out of any loyalty to the Nazis. On the other hand the possibility exists that he was assassinated either by loyal Nazis who wanted to keep him quiet, or by their enemies who took a final measure of revenge.

CHRONOLOGY
OF THE LIFE OF
RUDOLF VON SEBOTTENDORFF

1875   (November 9) born Adam Alfred Rudolf Glauer in Hoyerswerda in Saxony

1893   (June) his father dies

1897   (October 1) reports for obligatory military service, rejected for health reasons

1898   (March) private tutor in Hannover

            (April 2) begins work in merchant shipping as technician

1900   in Australia prospecting for gold

            (early July) meets Hussain Pasha in Alexandria

            (late July) travels from Alexandria to Constantinople (Istanbul)

            (October) begins a one-year contract to work for Hussain on an estate near Bursa, meets Termudi and is initiated into a mystical lodge

1901   returns to Germany

1902–03   resides in Munich

1905   (March 25) marries Karla Voss

1907   (May 5) divorces Karla

1908   returns to Constantinople (Istanbul)

1909   in Constantinople during counter-revolution of Sultan Hamid II; involved in German court case

1910	(December) founds a mystical lodge in Constantinople
1911	becomes a Turkish citizen, adopted by German expatriate Baron Heinrich von Sebottendorff
1912–13	active with the Red Crescent in the Balkan War, wounded, and briefly captured
1913	returns to Germany, resides in Berlin
1914	repeated adoption by Siegmund von Sebottendorff von der Rose, leaves Germany for Austria
1915	(July 15) marries Berta Anna Iffland in Vienna, later returns to Germany
1916	lives in Bad Aibling in Bavaria, joins the Germanen Order (September), visits with Hermann Pohl, head of the Germanen Order in Berlin
1917	recruited for the Bavarian branch of the GO
	(December) becomes publisher of GO publication
	selected master of GO Bavarian province
1918	(April 17) Thule Society ceremonially founded
	(July) meetings of the GO begin at Hotel Vierjahreszeiten in Munich; Thule Society used as a cover-name
	(July) buys the Franz Eher Verlag and the *Beobachter*, renamed *Münchner Beobachter*
	(October) Arbeiterverein formed within the Thule, later fashioned into a political party: Deutsche Arbeiter Partei

(November 7) bloodless coup of Socialists in Bavaria

(November 9) delivers political speech against the Socialists at the Thule meeting

(November) stockpiles weapons for counter-revolution

1919   (January 5) German Workers' Party formally founded

formation of Thule militia

(April 6) anarchists proclaim the Bavarian Socialist Republic

(April 13) Communists seize power in Bavaria

(April 26) Communists take seven Thule members hostage

(April 30) Thule members executed in basement of Liutpold School

(June 22) attends his last Thule meeting

(July) leaves Munich for Switzerland

(May 1) white (anti-Communist) forces enter Munich, Thule militia already in action in the streets

Communists ousted

1920   (October) succeeds Ernst Tiede as editor of *Astrologische Rundschau* (Astrological Review)

1920–23   continues editing *Astrologische Rundschau,* lives mainly in Germany

1923   (Spring) leaves Germany for Lugano, Switzerland, where he writes *The Secret Practices of Sufi Freemasons*

1924   *The Secret Practices of Sufi Freemasons* published as *Die Praxis der alten türkischen Freimauerei*

       returns to Turkey

1926–28   acts as honorary Mexican Consul in Turkey

1929–31   travels to United States and Mexico

1933   returns to Germany to revive the Thule Society

       (December) the book *Bevor Hitler kam* (Before Hitler Came) published

1934   second edition of *Bevor Hitler kam* issued

       (March 1) *Bevor Hitler kam* banned and confiscated by the Nazi Party

       (January and March) briefly jailed by Nazi authorities

       returns to Turkey employed by the German Intelligence Service under Herbert Rittlinge in Istanbul

1944   (September) German embassy closes in Istanbul, Sebottendorff given funds for one year

1945   (May 9) likely commits suicide by jumping off a bridge into the Bosporus

WORKS AND IDEAS

Works

The life and legend of the adventurer known as the Baron Rudolf von Sebottendorff von der Rose is so fascinating and compelling that the more important and useful information about his teachings and thoughts are usually glossed over. We do not want to let that happen here. However, it must be admitted that discovering what the baron really thought can be a difficult task. This is because his did not write that much when compared to his contemporaries. Also what he wrote tended to be from different genres—for example, novels, histories of astrology, technical astrological texts, and the book on Sufi exercises.

When we look at Sebottendorff's written output we discover that most of it concerned aspects of the practice of astrology. His works include: *Die Hilfshoroskopie* (1921), *Stunden- und Frage-Horoskopie* (1921), *Sterntafeln (ephemeriden) von 1838–1922* (Star Tables [Ephemeris] from 1838 to 1922) (1922), and *Astrologisches Lehrbuch* (Astrological Textbook) (1927). Perhaps to be counted as his masterpiece in astrological studies is *Geschichte der Astrologie* (History of Astrology), vol. I (1923). No second volume appeared.

Besides these astrological works, three others stand out.

The first of these is our text, *Die Praxis der alten türkischen Freimauerei* (1924). Second is a novel, *Der Talisman des Rosenkreuzers* (The Talisman of the Rosicrucian) (1925). This is said to be a thinly veiled autobiographical account from which many events in his life are discernible. Finally there is the ill-fated *Bevor Hitler kam* (1933). The latter two books are in one way or another attempts to manipulate the reader's views of the author. Only in the *Praxis* does Sebottendorff really speak to the reader about his own philosophy—if only vaguely.

Sebottendorff's Ideology

Sebottendorff, the man, remains an enigma. Some of his writings were probably produced to achieve some specific political agenda that was not necessarily a creation of his own thoughts. However, if we read his words carefully we can arrive at some general ideas about the intellectual and spiritual cosmos in which he lived. In many respects Sebottendorff was the typical German of his time—a man with a split character: one part fierce nationalist, the other a lover of the exotic. In Sebottendorff's lifetime he had reason to be proud of being German—Germans were the best educated, most technologically advanced and economically developed of all European peoples. At the same time they loved exotic ideas and exotic cultures; they studied them, and traveled to them at an enormous rate. Even now, more Germans travel outside their own borders per year than any other nation, and it is not coincidence that the German word *wanderlust,* "a strong and irresistible impulse to travel," had to be borrowed into English.[3] All this accounts for Sebottendorff's German nationalism coupled with his love of Turkey. To understand his ideology, we must divide the political dimension from the occult aspect; although we will see some common ground between the two.

Political Ideology

Most of Sebottendorff's written output would not indicate much of an interest in politics. It is far more oriented toward occult matters. However, both his biography and one book in particular, *Bevor Hitler kam* (1933), show his involvement in founding and directing insurgent political operations. Where and how he came by these skills and interests remain mysterious.

In introductory sections of his 1933 book he describes his devotion to two ideas *Deutschtum* (Germanism) and socialism. The idea of *Deutschtum* had been current in Europe for many decades.[4] On the one hand it can be understood as simply nationalism. But German nationalism, as with other forms of this idea elsewhere in the Old World, is heavily tinged with racial ideas. German (or English or French or Russian) nationalism meant more than fanatically supporting a political state. It meant a belief that the culture of the nation, its language, ethnicity, customs, and aesthetics, were to be promoted to the exclusion of foreign or outside elements. It also was bound up with concepts of antimodernism. Antimodernists saw industrialization, commercialism, and democracy as destructive to the nation and to *Deutschtum*.

To some extent these ideas were rooted in the esoteric teachings of men such as Guido von List (1848–1919) who coined and popularized a good deal of the terminology connected with this idea. Clearly Sebottendorff was steeped in the teachings of von List and others. But he was far from being alone in this. In fact List was himself merely another product of a larger neoromantic wave of ideology championed by Richard Wagner and others decades earlier.

The other political idea that moved Sebottendorff was *socialism*. Mainstream historical revisionism quickly moved to ignore the socialistic aspects of Hitler's National Socialism. It really should not be surprising therefore to see immediate precursors to Hitler extolling the idea of socialism, which most today think of in terms of left-wing politics. The essential theoretical factor that separates Hitler from Stalin was that the former saw biology or race as the decisive factor, while the latter saw economics and economic class as paramount. In practice, however, both essentially practiced nationalistic socialism under a dictatorship or oligarchy.

Certainly Sebottendorff, like many of his German and European contemporaries, envisioned a kinder and gentler form of socialism; one that wisely and benevolently collected the wealth and privilege of the nation and redistributed it to the benefit of the whole of society. Such dreams always lead immediately to a Hitler or Stalin, when applied on a national scale. National socialism would attempt to apply socialistic concepts and methods to the benefit of a single race or nationality—the Germans—rather than to an economic class—the proletariat—as is the case with the Marxists.

Occult Ideology

The occult encompasses ideas of a secret or hidden nature, which represent rejected patterns of thought (e.g., paganism, astrology, alchemy, magic) or concepts that have not been accepted by mainstream and established intellectual authorities (e.g., UFOs, ESP, orgone). Such ideas may be entirely taboo in a society and forced into secret societies, or they may simply be marginalized. Despite its outsider status the realm of the occult often becomes the breeding ground for revolutionary ideas.

Sebottendorff's occult ideology can be partially reconstructed from his works. One factor of great importance to him was a sort of unified field of reality that connected things such as the stars with the fate and character of individual humans. Here we see an echo of the Islamic insistence on the essential unity of being (the Arabic *wahdat-al-wujûd*). This also provides Sebottendorff with the rationale for his focus on tradition and national traditions—whether in Germany or Turkey. Such a unity of being also provides for the plausibility of alchemy. The base and the noble are, after all, parts of the same whole, or substance. Therefore the transmutation of one thing to another is theoretically possible, without changing the nature of reality.

One of Sebottendorff's chief themes is the idea of the perfectibility of the individual. This is the root concept behind the exercises belonging to the science of the key, as the ancient practice of Freemasonry is sometimes known. The fruits of this labor should, however, be transferred to the larger society in which the individual lives and this doctrine of perfectibility spread throughout the country. This, we are told, is the original mission of this book. The individual can, in a manner of speaking, become something akin to a philosopher's stone. His presence can act as a catalyst for widespread transformation. Is this the secret of Sebottendorff? So much power and influence has been ascribed to him, yet the facts of his life do not reflect such a man. How could a relatively unknown occultist and adventurer exert such historical influence and fade from the scene years before the results of his operation were manifest? Why then did he come back to make a conspicuous return at the moment of the operation's dark triumph, before once more fading into obscurity? Is all of this a testimony to the power of these exercises? Were these exercises at the root of other men's power, men from Muhammad to Hassan-i-Sabbah to Sebottendorff?

Certainly another of Sebottendorff's principal ideas was that individuals are capable of creating and re-creating their own environment. This concept was juxtaposed to the modernistic idea that individuals are products of their environments. All of this again brings forth Sebottendorff's essentially magical and alchemical view of man's capacity. The human being, and especially the individual who has been empowered by the secret practices revealed in the science of the key, can take active control of life and environment—but only in accordance with the will and direction of God.

2

The Bektashi Sect
of Sufism

ISLAM

In order to understand the Bektashi sect of Sufism and its
place in the work of the science of the key, we must come to
some understanding of the history and ideas of both Islam
and Sufism in general. Islam is obviously considered one of
the world's great religions. It now claims approximately one
and a half billion adherents worldwide. Just over fifty countries, stretching from Morocco to Indonesia, have Islam as
their official religion. As a religion it has spread farther and
faster than any known to history. Its founder, Muhammad
(567–632), personally oversaw the conquest and conversion
of his native Arabia. During his lifetime, he dictated texts
that were written down as the *Qur'an* (recitation); edited and
compiled some nineteen years after the death of the Prophet.

The essence of Islam is submission of the will to God, for the very word *islam* means "submission" in Arabic. The most essential doctrines of Islam are the Five Pillars of Faith: (1) the *shalât,* the practice of five daily prayers and prostrations; (2) the *zakât,* or obligatory almsgiving; (3) *sawn,* which is fasting from dawn to dusk during the month of *Râmâdan;* (4) *hajj,* or pilgrimage to Mecca; and (5) the *shahâdat,* or profession of faith—"There is no God but Allah, and Muhammad is his Prophet." This makes Islam originally and essentially simpler than Judaism or Christianity. Performing these obligatory practices is the core of Islam as originally practiced.

Historically, Islam spread out from Arabia in the wake of military conquests to the east and west of the Arabian Peninsula. Egypt fell in 641, and by 711 Muslims had invaded the European continent and conquered Visigoth Spain. The vast Persian Empire was brought into the Islamic world between 650 and 750 CE. Around the year 1000 Muslims made significant inroads into India; from there Islam staged further expansions eastward.

From early times in the history of Islam the religion was practiced by many non-Arabic peoples—most notably Persians. The Persians were among the world's most intellec-tual and sophisticated peoples at the time they were conquered by the relatively unlearned Bedouin Arabs. Persian cultural influence, already great in Arabia for centuries, would play a key role in the rapidly developing Islamic intellectual culture of the eighth and ninth centuries.

The Turkic peoples had generally converted to Islam by the ninth century. They are a non-Arabic, originally nomadic group of peoples originally inhabiting regions in central and northern Asia. During the eleventh century they made significant conquests in Asia Minor against the Byzantine Empire, which the Muslims called *Rûm*, or Rome. The Seljuk Turks' taking of Jerusalem from the Arabs and their victory over Byzantium at the Battle of Manzikert in 1071 marked the beginning of a Turkish onslaught on Europe—which reached its peak in 1683 at the Battle of Vienna. Here the Turks were defeated and turned back from the heart of central Europe. By this time the Ottoman Turks had conquered the entire Balkan region of Europe, including present-day Greece. In practical military and strategic terms, it was against the beginning of this invasion that the so-called Crusades were originally aimed. Christendom was under attack in the west (Spain) and in the east (Balkans), and the response was to counterattack the Holy Land. Following initial successes under the Normans beginning in 1098, the Crusades eventually collapsed after repeated campaigns, and the Christians were eventually pushed out of the region in 1291.

These two centuries of conflict between Christendom and Islam, which still leave their marks upon contemporary history, had one unintended consequence—the exposure of Christians to Islamic ideas and culture. Similarly, Islamic ideas entered into Christendom from the west in Spain. These ideas were philosophical (the Muslims had preserved Greek philosophy and science at a level unknown in Europe), scientific, technological, mathematical, as well as mystical, and even romantic. The Muslims also enjoyed many luxuries that wealthy Europeans wanted. Christian secular lords and the kings and their knights who fought in the Crusades knew and respected their enemies, unlike the religious fanatics who saw in Islam only a form of devil worship. It was through these secular doors that Islamic technology, magic, and mysticism entered into Europe.

The secret of Islamic advancement was its originally lax attitude toward individual thought. As long as a man met his religious obligations, he was free to think about a wide variety of things—as long as it did not lead to outward questioning of Islam, the Prophet, or the supremacy of his book, the *Holy Qur'an*. In the medieval West, by contrast, there was official religious control on virtually every aspect of philosophy, art, science, and all venues of culture. Islamic intellectual freedom preserved its cultural and military supremacy for centuries.

At the dawn of the western Modern Age, just before 1500 CE, things began to shift. There was a renaissance of pagan, or pre-Christian, philosophy in Europe. The Muslims were eventually pushed back out of Europe. The Spanish completed their reconquest of their country in 1492 and the Turks were left with only one small foothold in Europe around Constantinople (Istanbul). Increasingly the Muslims were seized by a religious fundamentalism, exemplified by the Wahhabist sect, and they lost their intellectual edge. It was during this period that the balance of intellectual and scientific power shifted from the Islamic superiority to European secular superiority. This shift is again seminal to understanding our times. Sadly the Islamic world went from being the richest and most advanced culture in the world to one of relative poverty and cultural deprivation.

To illustrate this shift it has been noted that if the economic impact of petroleum is removed from economic calculations dealing with the fifty or so Islamic countries, all of them together would have a combined gross domestic product less than that of any one of several small northern European countries.

SUFISM

Sufism is the best known esoteric or mystical dimension within the religion of Islam. Its definition is difficult, its origins obscure, and its history is fraught with contradictory sects and teachings. Sebottendorff purported to represent the esoteric practice of one order within the larger Sufi world— that of the Bektashis. But in order to grasp the importance of this, a general overview of Sufism is needed.

The word *sufi* is most likely derived from *suf,* the Arabic word for wool, and is a reference to the woolen garments early adherents of these doctrines wore as insignia. Supposedly, members of Muhammad's own entourage were among the earliest of the Sufis; for example, Selman, Muhammad's Persian barber, whom he had adopted. In general, Sufism may be defined as a mystical branch of Islam that seeks direct and personal knowledge and experience of God. This is opposed to the simple acceptance of the Qur'an and obedience to the laws of outward Islamic practice.

Because Islam arose and spread through many lands, each with its own religious and mystical traditions, it would be difficult to imagine that these would not have left their marks in the Islamic culture over the centuries. Sufism becomes the general feature of Islamic culture that was capable of absorbing spiritual ideas, teachings, and practices from other cultures as they were being politically annexed in the expansion of Islam. These influences came from such diverse sources as Christianity, Neoplatonism, Manichaeism, Zoroastrianism, Buddhism, and Hinduism. The latter-day Bektashi sect into which Sebottendorff was initiated may have been largely eclectic and universalistic, however, in this it is carrying on an ancient tradition of bringing together disparate practices into an Islamic or Sufi context.

As might be imagined there were many often cross-fertilizing orders of Sufism in the Middle Ages. The earliest phase of Sufism was characterized by its asceticism; for example, the teachings of

Hasan al-Basrî (died 728 CE) or Ibrâhim bin Adham of eastern Iran (died 777 CE).[1] Following this there were a multitude of Sufi masters who seem to have arisen in Iran. It seems that they often came from the easternmost part of the region, beyond the Oxus River. Not all of the early Iranian Sufis were very orthodox in their views, in fact Hussayn-ibn-Mansur al-Hallâj was executed for his teachings.[2] Another Iranian, Al-Ghazzâlî (died 1111) is credited with healing the rift between Sufism and orthodoxy.[3] This ushered in the greatest age of Sufism exemplified by Ibn Arabî (1165–1240), the Persian Shihâboddin Yahajâ Suhrawardî (1155–1191), and Muhammad Jalâl al-Din, better known as Rûmî (the Roman) (1207–1273). The second of these met the same fate as Al-Hallâj—martyrdom for his beliefs. The last of these, Rûmî, is one of the most popular figures produced by Islam. He founded a Sufi order (*târiqa*) in Asia Minor, which eventually became known, in Turkish, as the Mevlâna Order. These are the famous whirling dervishes.

THE BEKTASHI ORDER

A contemporary of Rûmî, Haji Bektash Veli (1209–1271), was from Nishpur in northeastern Iran and was driven from his home by Mongol invasions when they went to Asia Minor. There he founded a sect of Sufis that bears his name, the Bektashis. They were part of the Alevi movement in Asia

Minor, the members of which worship in assembly houses (Turkish *cemevi*), have ceremonies including music and dance, conduct rituals together with women, and use vernacular languages (not necessarily Arabic) for philosophical discourse and poetry. The Alevi movement is marked by its spirit of tolerance and egalitarianism.

Over time the Bektashi openness to outside influences made it a ready-made tool for cultural and mystical syncretism.

Another essential piece in the puzzle presented by the contents of Sebottendorff's book is the role of Hurufism in the Bektashi *tariqat*. Hurufism means "letterism." The founder of the Hurufis was the Persian Fazlallah Astarabadi (1340–1394), who wrote in his native language under the name Naimi. He, as was the case with several other Sufi pioneers, was martyred by orthodox interests. It is the basic idea of Hurufism that God reveals himself in the word, and that the word is made up of sounds or letters with accompanying numerical values. These are made manifest in the human body through certain exercises. One who has gained proficiency in this may be able to act in a godlike manner.

Additionally, we can recognize influences from the Qalandariyya Order founded by Yusuf al-Andalusi (died 1070) in Spain. This order is marked by antinomian practices, the consumption of intoxicants, and the use of gambling and games. It also practices something called *shahed bâzî*, "witness play," which involves in part the contemplation of the beauty of the human body.

The Bektashi Order was the official sect of the Turkish Janissaries—an elite fighting force within the Turkish army made up of originally non-Muslim boys who fell into Turkish hands. The Janissaries were active from 1365 to 1826 when they were disbanded due to the great influence they had gained in Turkish politics. During their long history the Janissaries were most prominent in the Balkan region.

It appears that over time the Bektashi sect or order developed in two directions, with some embracing the more heretical aspects of the order more than others. This has led to a general opinion or feeling among more orthodox Muslims that there are bad Bektashis and good ones. In some versions, however, *all* Bektashis are bad. In fact, of course, it is merely a matter of historical development. One thing that appears to enrage orthodox Muslims the most is that the so-called bad Bektashis accept even Jews among them. The fact that the Termudi clan who befriended Sebottendorff were Jews speaks to the fact that these were indeed the bad Bektashis. Some Bektashis have embraced not only Alevi practices, but that of Hurufism, as well. It should be noted that in 1925 Kamal Ataturk banned all Sufi orders as a part of secularizing the nation of Turkey. Due to their nature, however, such orders survived and later resurfaced unscathed.

3

The Mysteries of the
Arabic Letters

The very idea of writing has tremendous power and influence in a culture. Humans have been writing for somewhat over five thousand years, yet many remain illiterate—even in Islamic countries with their overwhelming reverence for the book. The Arabs of Muhammad's time were generally illiterate, as he was himself. Arabic writing was largely developed to record his recitations—the Qur'an.

We see that many traditional cultures resisted becoming literate. The Brahmans of India resisted for centuries. Caesar says of the Druids that they would not write down their sacred teachings, because the concepts would be profaned by writing. The Germanic peoples used a form of writing for more than a millennium—the runes—before ever using them for overtly profane texts. Writing can eventually have the effect of demystifying language, and thus further impoverish the human spirit. Robert Logan in his book *The Alphabet Effect* points to thought features such as "abstraction, analysis, rationality, and classification"[1] as the essence of this effect on those who learn to use a phonetic script. This is especially true of later users of the script. Early practitioners of writing were, as we have noted, often somehow aware of what might be lost in the absorption of such a profound tool. For this reason extralinguistic (often mystical, religious, or magical) traditions were developed to keep the mystery of language alive. We clearly see this in the Islamic world, but it is also apparent when we look at the Greek alphabet, the Germanic runes, and perhaps most familiarly the Hebrew tradition of Kabbalah.

The Arabic writing system is based upon that of the Old Semitic tradition to which the Hebrew script also belongs. The names of the letters go back to a Canaanite source, but the Arabic names do not originally convey any meaning beyond merely being abstract names for the letters. The letter names do later take on secondary meanings. The ordering of the letters is also originally unique to the Arabic tradition, and not based on the Old Semitic tradition. For esoteric purposes the letters have at times been rearranged to reflect the older tradition.

The script appears to have been adapted from the Kufic

writing system for use in transcribing the text of the Qur'an. The first such transcriptions were made on various objects in the Prophet's lifetime, so tradition tells us. These were codified into a fixed text by about two decades after Muhammad's death in the seventh century, although the oldest surviving actual manuscripts date from about a century later. Oddly the chapters, or *suras,* were arranged from the longest to the shortest. As regards the mysterious "abbreviated letters" (Arabic *muqatta'at*) we cannot know for certain that they were originally part of the text or a somewhat later addition. However, they were present in the oldest extant manuscripts.

To the Muslim the Qur'an is more than a book. A translation of the Qur'an is not the Qur'an. It is only a *holy* book when written in Arabic. Almost all Muslims, regardless of what their native language is, use Arabic as a liturgical language for prayer, and the Qur'an is written in Arabic with Arabic letters.

The Arabic writing system came to be used to represent many of the languages of the peoples the Islamic Arabs conquered—either militarily or diplomatically. Persian adapted the Arabic by adding a few letters to represent sounds not found in Arabic. Hindustani (Urdu) followed suit. Turkic languages similarly adopted the Arabic script—although most of them now use either forms of the Roman or Cyrillic (Russian) alphabet.

MYSTICAL MEANINGS OF
ARABIC LETTERS

Besides the tradition of the abbreviated letters which we will explore in some detail below, there are many widespread teachings concerning the mystical meanings of the Arabic letters among Muslims—especially in Sufi orders, of course.

When approaching the science of letters (Arabic *'ilm âl-Huruf* or *'ilm-âl-abjad*) it is most fundamental to know that an Arabic letter is made up of three basic levels:

1. Shape
2. Sound
3. Number

Any interpretation or meaning derives from mystical traditions involving these elements. From a religious point of view the letters make up the parts of the word of God by which he creates and shapes the universe.

The symbolism of the moon has always been important to Islam. It so happens that the twenty-eight phases or mansions of the moon are reflected in the fact that there are twenty-eight letters in the Arabic alphabet. There are twenty-nine if we count the *hamza*. It is also true that there are twenty-nine suras that have the abbreviated letters attached to them. These matters are unlikely to be coincidences. There is no one explanation of these things in Islamic tradition, but many Sufi teachers have used these features in their philosophies and practices. We only offer some of these ideas to illustrate the richness of Muslim letter symbolism, of which the science of the key to the abbreviated letters is only one part.

MYSTIC INTERPRETATIONS OF THE ARABIC LETTERS

In the following sections the twenty-nine Arabic letters will be depicted followed by a standard transcription in the Roman alphabet, the name of the letter and it numerical values, and the set of abbreviated letters said to correspond to that letter. Then there are other symbolic or mystical attributes ascribed to the letter. Regarding the numerical values that appear in parentheses, the first is the value according to the normal or Moroccan system, and the second is that according to the Egyptian system, which reflects a tradition more in line with other Semitic alphabetic numerology.

 A *alif* (1/1) ALM (sura 2) Divine aspects ascribed to *A*: divine essence, the first, the intellect, the pen

ﺏ B *bâ* (2/2) ALM (sura 3) Aspects of God attributed to *B* are the subtle, the jinn

ﺕ T *tâ* (3/400) HM (sura 41) Attributes of God corresponding to *T* are the reckoner, the one who causes contraction, the sphere of ether, and meteors

ﺙ Th *tha* (4/500) HM OSQ (sura 42) Divine and cosmic aspects ascribed to *Th* are the one who nourishes and the planets

ﺝ J *jim* (5/3) ALMS (sura 7) The aspects of God and cosmos linked to *J* are the independent and the heaven around the zodiac

ﺡ H *ha* (6/8) ALR (sura 14) Divine and cosmic attributes are the last and the universal substance

ﺥ Kh *ka* (7/600) HM (sura 43) Aspects of the divine and of the cosmos are the wise and the very idea of form

ﺩ D *dal* (8/8) ALR (sura 10) Aspects of the cosmos and of the divine include: the evident, the seventh heaven, the moon, and the abode of Adam

ذ Dh *dhal* (9/4) HM (sura 44) Attributes of the divine and of the order of the world are the one who humbles and the animals

ر R *ra* (10/200) S (sura 38) Divine and cosmic correspondences are the giver of forms, the fifth heaven, Venus, and the abode of Joseph

ز Z *za* (20/7) ALMR (sura 13) The corresponding name of God translates as the living and the cosmic link is air

س S *sin* (30/60) ALM (sura 29) The divine attribute is the one who gives life and the cosmic correspondence is water

ش Sh *shin* (40/300) HM (sura 40) The divine correspondence is called the powerful and the cosmic link is with the heaven of the fixed stars

ص S *sad* (50/90) ALM (sura 32) The attribute of God is the one who lays and the cosmic correspondence is Earth

ض D *dad* (60/800) HM (sura 45) The divine name is the knowing and the cosmic attributes are the second heaven, Jupiter, and the abode of Moses

ط T *ta* (70/9) HM (sura 41) The divine attribute is the reckoner and the cosmic correspondences are the sixth heaven, Mercury, and the abode of Jesus

ظ Z *za* (80/900) HM (sura 46) The attribute of God here is the precious and the cosmic meaning is metals and minerals

ع *'ayn* (90/70) ALM (sura 30) The divine attribute is the hidden and the cosmic concept is universal nature

غ Gh *ghain* (100/1000) Q (sura 50) The corresponding name of God is the manifest and the cosmic meaning is universal body

ف F *fa* (200/80) ALM (sura 31) The name of God is the strong and the cosmic link is the Angels

ق Q *qaf* (300/100) YS (sura 36) Here the divine attribute is the one who encompasses all and the cosmic meaning is the throne

ك K *kaf* (400/20) TH (sura 20) The divine attribute is the grateful while the cosmic meaning is the pedestal

ل L *lam* (500/30) TSM (sura 26) The name of God here is the victorious and the cosmic meanings are the third heaven, Mars, and the abode of Aaron

م M *mim* (600/40) TS (sura 27) The divine attribute is the one who gathers and the cosmic significance is man

ن N *nun* (700/50) TSM (sura 28) Here the name of God is the light and the cosmic meanings are the fourth heaven, the sun, and the abode of Hermes

ه H *ha* (800/5) ALR (sura 11) The divine attribute is the one who calls forth, while the cosmic correspondences are the universal soul and the guarded tablet

و W *waw* (900/6) ALR (sura 12) Here the divine attribute is the one who possesses sublime degrees and the cosmic commentary is the hierarchical degrees of existence, not their manifestation

ي Y *ya* (1000/10) KHYOS (sura 19) The name of God is the Lord and the cosmic correspondences are the first heaven, Saturn, and the abode of Abraham

ء *hamza* (no numerical value) N (sura 68) This falls

outside of Ibn Arabî's cosmological system, but is a part of the science of the key

If these letters are rearranged in the so-called secret, or Egyptian, order, the number of the sura to which each set of abbreviated letters corresponds will be sequential.

There have been many such descriptions of the symbolic meanings of Arabic letters over the centuries; their authority depends upon one's faith in the particular teacher whose insight the descriptions represent. There is certainly no orthodox standard. This list represents the teachings of Ibn Arabî as found in his treatise on astrology.[2] To this list has been added the transcription of the abbreviated letters that figure so prominently in Sebottendorff's book. We will return to these in their own section below.

THE ABBREVIATED LETTERS

Among the mysteries of the Qur'an few are greater than that of the muqatta'at, or abbreviated letters. Many theories have been generated over the centuries to explain them. None is universally accepted, and the orthodox or conservative Muslim theologians refuse to accept any one theory over the others. They prefer to designate them as being inscrutable *mysteries.*

One article to be found on the Internet (http://thedisconnectedletters.wordpress.com) describes eleven different theories purporting to explain the muqatta'at, without even mentioning the one found in this book. More common theories as to their meaning include that they are mnemonic devices summarizing the contents of a given sura, that they are aids for ordering the text of the Qur'an, that they are orthographic examples of how to write certain letters, that they are names of the editors of the sura, or that they indicate how the sura is to be recited. Other more mystical explanations are that only Allah knows what they mean, that they have numerical or numerological significance, that they allude to Egyptian hieroglyphics, or that they are mystical signs of unknown significance. Apparently these letters have been a matter of speculation for centuries. Most of this speculation, however, appears in writings in Arabic, Persian, or Urdu. It is known that various Sufi orders, as well as the Baha'i religion, have school- or sect-specific interpretations. The theory presented in this book can only purport to be one such example. It does have the advantage of being a theory with a very focused and unified purpose. Many of the other theories start out as plausible *concepts,* but seem to break down in the specifics as far as their consistency is concerned.

Muqatta'at in the Qur'an

Serious discussions of the abbreviated letters cannot dispense with a description of them as they appear in the text of the Qur'an. Historically the muqatta'at were present in the Qur'an from its first edition made by the Calif Uthman around 653. It is unclear who is responsible for their presence. Abbreviation of known phrases was common in early Arabic literature, but the possibilities for interpreting the abbreviated letters in this way are too vast and too arbitrary to be very meaningful.

The following facts about the abbreviated letters leave little doubt that their meanings are intimately connected to the structure of the Arabic writing system itself. There are twenty-eight or twenty-nine letters in the Arabic alphabet, depending on whether the hamza is counted. Fourteen different letters occur in the list of the abbreviated letters:

H	K	S	A
Y	L	T	H
M	O	R	
N	Q	S	

Fourteen is, of course, exactly half of twenty-eight. The abbreviated letters occur at the beginnings of twenty-nine different suras. The table on page 42 shows the fourteen different combinations of abbreviated letters.

Muqatta'at	Sura
SA	38
QA	50
NA	68
TA HA	20
TAS	27
YAS	36
	40
	41
	42
HAM	43
	44
	45
	46
	2
	3
ALAM	29
	30
	31
	32
	10
	11
ALAR	12
	14
	15
TASAM	26
	27
ALAMAS	7
ALAMAR	13
KAHAY'S	19
HAM 'OSAQ	42

Note: The spellings on the above list are the more standard transcriptions. Those on page 68 are the spellings given by Sebottendorff in this text.

In the Qur'an, the *alif* (A) occurs in these formulas written as a horizontal line above the letter or letters (ā). This makes the formulas into pronounceable forms and shows how, for example, the basic formula "alm" becomes "alam." This indicates that the formulas could be pronounced as depicted in Sebottendorff's text (see page 68).

Most of these formulas are easy enough to pronounce. The only difficulties posed for English speakers are the glottal stop 'O represented by the letter *'ein*, transliterated here as 'O, and the *Q* (*qaf*). The glottal stop is a pause in speech. It occurs, for example, in Cockney English *water*, pronounced *wa'er*. The sound of the *qaf* is made by pronouncing *k*, but farther back and down in the throat.

Possible Symbolic Meanings of the Muqatta'at

In his monumental translation of the Qur'an, A. Yusuf Ali offers some notes on the possible meanings of the abbreviated letters. He, like most orthodox commentators, insists that these interpretations are only conjectural and that the ultimate meanings of these mysterious signs remain unknowable.

ALM   This refers to the mystery of the beginning and the end, the past and the future, life and death.

ALMS   This formula is the *ALM* plus the letter *S*, which indicates that the sura in question contains a narrative or story that illustrates the principle of *ALM*.

ALMR   Ali comments: "Here there seems to be a combination of the groups ALM and ALR. We consider here not only the beginnings (A), the middle (L) and the end (M) of man's spiritual history, but also the immediate future of the interior of our organization . . ."[3]

KHYOS   It is thought that the first four letters refer to the names of the various prophets mentioned in sura 19, which is the only one with these muqatta'at. The final *S* indicates the presence of stories about these prophets.

TH   With the vowels this reads: *ta ha,* and is an interjection meaning "oh, man!" This refers to the subject of the sura, Moses, who is in spiritual crisis.

TSM   Yusuf Ali is not satisfied with this interpretation, but it seems common to interpret these letters as referring to Tur-i-Sînîn (Mount Sinai), plus the name Moses. This is the theme of suras 26 and 28.

TS   If the *TSM* interpretation is true, then *TS* simply refers to Mount Sinai.

YS   *Ya sin* is considered a mystic title of the Prophet Muhammad.

S   The interpretation of this letter as meaning stories or narratives, which occurs in the formulas *ALMS* and *KHYOS*, fits here insofar as the content of sura 38 has to do with stories about David and Solomon.

HM   This occurs in a series of seven suras (40–46). Their common theme is a juxtaposition of good to evil, faith to unfaith.

Q   Yusuf Ali cites the interpretation that this stands for the Arabic phrase *Qudhiya-amru,* "the matter has been decreed." This reflects the eschatological content of sura 50, to which it is prefixed.

N   The letter name *nûn* can mean fish or an ink holder in Arabic. The fact that the Pen or *Nûn* is also the title of this sura (68) strengthens this interpretation.

HM 'OSK   This unique combination appears only before sura 42. It is among a series of *HM* chapters. The significance of *'OSK* is obscure.

In our description of the mystical meanings of the Arabic letters derived from the teachings of Ibn Arabî appeared descriptions of the Quranic muqatta'at to each of the individual letters. Again, that is just one more order- or sect-specific teaching. But the fact that the number of uses of the abbreviated letters and the number of letters in the Arabic alphabet coincide is likely to be significant.

The overriding and abiding truth about the abbreviated letters is that they are, and remain *mysteries*. Most of the attempts to make sense of them presented in this section are based to one degree or another on rational thought and in-depth analysis leading to some sort of esoteric insight. The Bektashi doctrine in Sebottendorff's work takes another approach. It bypasses—in true Sufi fashion—the rational phase altogether. It simply instructs the practitioner to *do*— and to receive esoteric knowledge (*gnosis*) and spiritual development directly. It speaks of using mystic signs or gestures to unravel the mysteries contained in written texts and symbols. In other words the poles are reversed here. The irrational and directly experiential unravels the mysteries contained in intellectual material. Nothing of what has been said about the possible symbolic content of the Arabic letters or of the muqatta'at matter at all. The abbreviated letters cannot be understood or analyzed by the rational mind. They are put there to be *used*. They are irrational keys embedded in the text of the Qur'an in order to preserve them for eternity, without betraying their mysteries. As such, although most intellectual attempts to explain the abbreviated letters spend a good deal of effort to remain religiously orthodox, the most unorthodox approach may be the one that takes the sentiment of religious commentators most to heart—that the muqatta'at are mysteries known only to Allah and revealed to Muhammad.

4

Alchemy and Sufism

Alchemy as it became known in the late Middle Ages and Renaissance times in Europe is clearly an influence felt directly from the Muslim world. The word itself is derived from Arabic *al-kimiyâ,* "the art of transmutation." This was borrowed into Arabic from the Greek χημεια (*khêmeia*), "the (Egyptian) art of transmutation." The art was ascribed to Egypt, although most evidence for what became known as alchemy is derived from Greek sources generated in Alexandria and Harran, a place in the east to which pagan philosophers in Greece fled when the Christians closed their schools.

A quasi-mythical figure named Jabîr ibn Hayyân (known in the West as Geber), who might be a conglomerate persona made up from several Muslim writers on alchemy and magic, lived sometime in the eighth to tenth century. Arabic works on alchemy began to be translated into Latin around 1150. Sufi masters such as Mansûr al-Hallaj, Aviccena, and Ibn Arabî emphasized the spiritual dimension of the alchemical art.

In alchemy we essentially see an amalgamation of ancient Greek science and chemistry (using the primitive periodic table of Fire-Air-Earth-Water) and the attempt to transform the individual human being using esoteric techniques. If physical objects could be transmuted from one substance to another—if lead could be turned to gold—then the human soul could likewise be transformed from a base state into a noble, godlike state using analogous formulas.

In fact it is far more accurate to see no distinction between the so-called physical and spiritual transmutations because both of these apparent categories of being belong to the same unity. Physical gold and perfection of the spiritual being are both reflections of a single higher symbol—the light. This idea, quite esoteric in the West, was well prepared for in the Islamic world with its essential doctrine of the oneness of being (Arabic *wahdat-al-wujûd*). Within the overarching context, outer physical manipulations and inner spiritual processes can be understood as equivalents.[1]

So when Sebottendorff writes of medieval alchemical processes in conjunction with the science of the key, he is perfectly within the bounds of historical possibilities. The well-known writer on Sufism, Idries Shah, in his book *The Sufis,* outlines several examples of Sufi knowledge passing into medieval Christendom.[2]

The Templars are most likely among the Western institutions influenced by the Sufis. Legend has it that they discovered something linking themselves to the mysteries of
Solomon in their excavations of the Temple Mount, at which
they had their headquarters in Jerusalem. That anything
would remain undiscovered after almost five hundred years
of Islamic occupation of Jerusalem and the Temple Mount
seems historically unlikely. Muslims conquered Jerusalem
in 638 and the Templars were established in 1120. What
is more likely is that the Knights Templar encountered living repositories of wisdom among the Muslims from whom
they learned secret teachings. Such a theory would explain a
good deal, including the basis for some of the charges brought
against them in 1307, which led to their official destruction.

ALCHEMY EAST AND WEST

The alchemical methods found in Sebottendorff's *The
Practice of Ancient Turkish Freemasonry* remind one of the
Chinese and Indic methods found in Taoist alchemy and
yoga practices.[3] Some have thought that these traditions represented Arabic influence in these Eastern cultures, but this is
probably not the case. Alchemical texts in the East date from
as early as the first millennium BCE, so it is obvious that the
pagan traditions of Egypt and Greece passed into these cul-

tures along the trade routes from a very early date. Islamic alchemy is the culmination of a long process, which in turn gave rise to a new cycle of interest in this art in the West.

In Chinese alchemy we see a clear tradition of interiorizing the alchemical process within a symbolic human physiology. Breath work in which a vital element is circulated between heaven, located in the head, and earth, located in the lower abdomen, with an intermediary level in the heart, or center, is a fundamental part of Chinese alchemy. The end product is an individual possessed of an immortal spirit body.

These ideas were probably introduced into China from India. There we find a refined esoteric human physiology— for example, the doctrine of *chakras,* connected with the practice of yoga. Again the exercises of yoga are intended to produce an immortal body and a perfected being.

In the East the interiorized symbolism is obvious and expressed as such. Perhaps this is because the authors were not trying to hide their intentions or the nature of their teachings from disapproving eyes. In the West, however, most alchemical texts always appear to be dealing with some exterior manipulation of material substances. Thus they often concealed their true meaning. The Sufi tradition represented by Sebottendorff in *The Practice of Ancient Turkish Freemasonry* is not trying to hide anything. However, its fundamental theory remains obscure to the noninitiate.

THEORY OF MYSTICAL ALCHEMY

It has long been recognized that the alchemical process was often aimed toward personal transformation and that the instrument was not a piece of technical apparatus, but the human body. The science of the key works in a miraculous way. The process is alchemical, but it is not forced by visualizations or overt intentions. It just happens if the formulas are applied as described. The process has a clear aim; a discernible model and method of operation leading to the stated aim of individual completion. Theory, as such, is relatively unimportant, although the various doctrines surrounding the rich traditions that inform the science of the key could keep theoretical thinkers busy for a lifetime.

The aim of the work is stated as being the spiritualization of matter, or in other words, the raw uneven stone is transformed into a cubical one. Sebottendorff continually refers to various metaphors for the purpose of the work being enlightenment and self-completion.

The model of operation used to achieve this goal can be fairly easily discerned. Obviously the body is seen as the instrument of the alchemical process. This is often completely obscure in Western descriptions of alchemy. Perhaps this is because the alchemists were attempting to conceal the true nature of their work, as it would rival the aims of religion itself. In the East, in China and India, the idea that the location of the alchemical operation is within the human body is often made overtly clear. In the case of the exercises presented by Sebottendorff it is obvious that the process occurs within the body of the practitioner. The laboratory instruments most easily compared to the function for the body in this process are the athanor and the alembic. The former is a sort of oven, with a fire below and a crucible in the middle with vapors rising to the upper levels of the instrument. An alembic is an instrument of distillation—the process by which, for example, alcohol is produced. The word *athanor* is derived from Arabic *al-tannur,* "oven." *Alembic* is similarly derived from an Arabic word, *al-anbiq,* which was borrowed from a Greek term αμβυξ (from *ambyx,* meaning "still"). In either case, energy (fire) is used to combine, mix, or separate basic substances and transforms them into something more subtle or spiritual.

The method of the practices of the ancient Turkish Freemasons demonstrates a similar process. The spirit is distilled from matter. This is done by drawing down and sealing off levels of energy in the esoteric circulatory system of the body by means of the formulas prescribed by the Quranic muqatta'at. The fact that these letters are used for this esoteric purpose is of the highest significance. In these formulas the whole power of the Book is contained and codified. They work in a miraculous fashion that does not require the alchemist to visualize or force phenomena to happen within his system. Rather the process happens as a matter of course if the instructions are followed exactly. In the practical sections of the text Sebottendorff lays out a clear and precise curriculum for attaining this goal according to a method he received from the Oriental Freemasons or Bektashi dervishes.

The Practice of Ancient Turkish Freemasonry

THE KEY TO THE
UNDERSTANDING OF ALCHEMY

*A Presentation of the Ritual, Doctrine, and Signs of
Recognition among the Oriental Freemasons*

Baron Rudolf von Sebottendorff

1924

Dedicated to the Memory of the Former Secretary
of the Turkish Embassy in Bern,
Mr. P. Schwidtal

Introduction

Libelli habeant sua fata*—the manuscript belongs to the book. The manuscript of this book had already been completed in another version at the beginning of the war,† but all sorts of opposing events prevented its appearance. Now a not completely voluntary stay in Switzerland is giving me the opportunity to revise the manuscript and prepare it for the press.

And it was good that the book did not appear earlier. Souls have become more receptive. There is one discovery after another now, and each is a deathblow to the materialistic philosophy and bogus monism. Just yesterday I read that they were successful in splitting the nitrogen atom, dividing it into hydrogen and helium.

---

*["Books are said to have their own destinies." —*Trans.*]
†[This refers to the First World War (1914–1918) —*Trans.*]

Those who have been paying attention to events in the Orient over the last few years must continually wonder in amazement: "How is it possible that a people such as the Turks, who aren't even a homogenous people, have been able to develop such perseverance, turn it against a world of enemies, and eventually carry it to victory? Anyone knowing how exhausted the people already were by the ongoing burdens of war, which only a Muslim can bear, when they entered the World War must also be amazed by their patience and endurance under the most difficult conditions. What is then the difference between Germany, which has almost had to succumb under the yoke of a horrendous peace, and Turkey, which rejected a similar peace and fought on to obtain different conditions?"*

The modern intellectual, schooled in materialism, will thanklessly strive to find the underlying reason for this because he is always focusing on externalities. He can in no way understand that it is the spiritual guidance and training alone, which every Muslim strives for from his youth forward, that have borne him through these hard times. We are experiencing

---

*[The Turkish Empire collapsed in September 1918, but quickly and forcefully reorganized itself as the Turkish Republic under the dictator Mustafa Kemal. The Turks resisted efforts by the allies to carve up the heartland of Turkey, and were even able to hold on to Constantinople/ Istanbul. — *Trans.*]

the shameful spectacle of a great part of the German people throwing themselves into the arms of the Bolsheviks expecting every sort of benefit from those who have declared materialism to be God, and we see that Turkey, this small, weakened land, certainly made use of the aid the Bolsheviks afforded them, but that they were far from throwing themselves into the arms of Bolshevism. On the contrary, it finds no place among them.

We see that one people, which had been counted as one of the most intellectually advanced, decided to take just such a step backward, while another people—previously scorned as being inferior—clearly recognized this step as ruinous and declined to participate, and not only rejected the step in its particulars, but in its entirety as well.

"Just tether your ass and commend it to God," goes a Turkish proverb. The West has always been of the belief that Islam is stagnant as a religion. Nothing is further from the truth; Islam is more viable than the Christian religion. It has proven its viability. The following exploration clearly shows us the wellspring of the power of Islam; it is up to us to make the wellspring useful to the Christian religion as well. It was living water from this wellspring that brought everything to fruition in the early period of the Church, and which pro-duced the most glorious flowering of the Middle Ages; only rationalism and materialism blocked this wellspring.

I will not be committing any sacrilege or profanation if

I reveal this wellspring. Whoever reads through this book attentively, and resolves to do the exercises shown here, can in no way misuse the powers acquired, for only the one who is upstanding, courageous, and determined will be able to persevere to the end and profit from the exercises. By profit I do not mean, of course, external success; that only makes its entrance when a person has become good in his very core.

The exercises of the Oriental Freemasons are nothing other than work on oneself, for ennobling, and for the acquisition of higher knowledge. From the subsequent explanations it will become clear that they contain the secret of the Rosicrucians and alchemists, and demonstrate the preparation of the stone, which is what the seeker is longing for.

I said: *Nothing other*—but that is the highest, the most unique thing that the seeker for knowledge can strive after. I will not require faith in my words from the reader, but rather I will prove my explanations. I will prove that Oriental Freemasonry authentically preserves to this day the ancient doctrines of wisdom, which modern Freemasonry has forgotten, for it must be said here at the beginning that the Freemasonic Constitution of 1717 was a detour from the right way.

Laws made from the outside cannot provide for the salvation of humanity. These laws are always being obliterated by other laws and are always having to be replaced by different laws—but rather it is the work from the inside out alone that can bring us salvation. Those who can consciously live according to the divine laws will perceive this as a duty, not as something coerced, and will act for the highest benefit of mankind, which will actually be the highest benefit to the individual as well. The divine laws are, however, absolutely unambiguous.

The only requirement I make of readers is that they be aware of their unity within God. Without this awareness the exercises are useless. Whoever still believes in the old monism, as propagated by Bückner and Haeckel, is just requested, if true knowledge is indeed being sought, to read without prejudice an opponent of this view, such as Surya: *Wahrer und Falscher Monismus.**

And now go forth, you little book, the hour is auspicious. I began this introduction on the third of February 1924 at 12:30 midday at latitude 46° north and longitude 9° east. Righteously bring salvation to the multitude through true knowledge.

---

*[G. W. Surya is the pseudonym used by Demeter Georgievitz-Weitzer —*Trans.*]

Practice

Islam means submission; that is, submission to the will of God. The believer can just commend himself to the will of God simply because it is the will of God. He feels secure and does not ask why this is so or why that is different—he fulfills the divine law simply because it is the revealed law of God. He accepts his fate as being immutable and, at the most, attempts by means of prayer to implore for mercy from God when the burden becomes too great for him. But the sign of the true believer will consistently be that he does not ask for release from the burden, but rather for the strength to be able to bear it. "Lead us in the way of those who do not err," the Prophet prescribes to those who pray.

This faithful condition is what is most worthy to strive after according to all religious systems. Actually the one who is faithful is also the most happy, is the one the Prophet values most highly, and represents this as the only goal—and therefore this religion is called *Islam*.

Now, besides belief there is something else that makes it equally possible for a person to yield to his fate; it is no longer faith but knowledge—knowledge of the divine laws. The one who knows no longer fulfills this law blindly, but rather knowingly. The truly wise one is very near to the believer, but is superior to the believer.

The Prophet created a very wise institution to open the way to knowledge for everyone who truly seeks it. According to this system in the Qur'an he provided explicit signs that point the way to knowledge and that have to reveal the law of creation to one who gains knowledge from within one's own being. The highest form of knowledge will always lead the wise to yield to divine providence without complaint—that is, to Islam through knowledge.

In what follows we will concern ourselves with this path. How the Prophet himself came into possession of this knowledge is recounted in the form of the following legend.

Not far from Mecca there lived at the time of Muhammad an aged hermit, Ben Chasi, who was teaching the Prophet. When the lesson was over he gave him a metallic plate upon which were engraved formulas, the meaning of which the then thirty-year-old Prophet had just learned.

Soon thereafter the hermit died, but Muhammad kept on teaching the secret of these formulas in the most intimate circles. Abu Bekr, the first caliph, inherited the plate and the knowledge, which only spread within a small circle after the death of the Prophet: this is the secret knowledge of the Oriental Freemasons.

In order to ensure against the loss of the formulas the Prophet distributed them throughout the Qur'an according to a precise key. The key is known, and the formulas are preserved in the Qur'an, such that the possibility remains for reconstructing the system at any time.

The formulas are preserved in the so-called abbreviated letters,* the meaning of which is debated among orientalists as well as different commentators. Some are of the opinion that these letters are signatures. Individual suras certainly originated under highly variable conditions: the Prophet dictated some, others he recited while friends wrote them down, still others were recorded later from memory. When the suras were collected the letters that indicated the originator of the sura would have remained, but now without their meaning.

Some European scholars are of the view that these letters represent notes by the scribe. Thus ALM is supposed to

---

*[Arabic *Al-Muqatta'at*. See Ali, trans. *The Holy Qur'an*, 2nd ed., 118–20. —*Trans.*]

mean: *amara li muhamed*—"Muhammad commanded me to write."

Arabic commentators view these letters as holy abbreviations. Thus ALM mean: *allah latif madshid*—"God is good"—or as another thinks: *ana lahu alamu*—"I am the God who knows."

For others the letters are to be interpreted in a kabbalistic sense. Certainly all the suras in which these letters occur contain definite indications that they have something special to say.

The Arabic language, like all the Semitic languages, does not write the vowels. If one does not read these letters as such, but rather as words, they yield no meaning. For this reason people have been scratching their heads over the meaning of these letters. But in actuality these are the secret formulas concealed in the letters that someone who knows the truth can now easily read and pronounce. All of these formulas are compounds of the vowel *A* with one or several consonants.

Now the secret doctrine shows that the sura in which the formula occurs specifies the number of days in the system the given formula is to be practiced. The table of the Prophet appears on the next page.

The number of days results in twenty-five lunar months in which three days are missing. On these three days the one who was dedicated to these exercises was occupied doing something else, to which we will return later.

Number of the sura	Name of the sura	Formula
2	The Cow	**alam**
3	Amran's Family	**alam**
7	El Araf	**alamas**
10	Jonah	**alar**
11	Houd	**alar**
12	Joseph	**alar**
13	Thunder	**alamar**
14	Abraham	**alar**
15	A-hijr	**alar**
19	Mary	**kaha ya as**
20	Ta ha	**ta ha**
26	The Poet	**tasam**
27	The Ant	**tas**
28	The Narration	**tasam**
29	The Spider	**alam**
30	The Greeks	**alam**
31	The Wise	**alam**
32	Adoration	**alam**
36	Ya sin	**yas**
38	Sad	**sa**
40	The Believer	**cham**
41	Revelations Well Expounded	**cham**
42	Consultation	**cham asak**
43	Gold Adornments	**cham**
44	Smoke	**cham**
45	Kneeling	**cham**
46	Al ahqaf	**cham**
50	Qaf	**ka**
68	The Feather	**na**
822 days		14 different formulas

The formulas are present in twenty-nine suras. For those who do not know anything about astrology it is noted that astrology knows of twenty-eight mansions of the moon, which amounts to the twenty-nine-day synodical rotation of the moon. The Persian mystic Mahmud Shebisteri, a Mel Mevlevi dervish, says in the *gulshen ras:*

> *And because Cancer found itself related to the*
>   *Moon*
> *It bound itself by head and tail to the Moon*
> *Through stations twenty-eight goes its course*
> *It positions itself in opposition to the Sun's light*
> *Then it shrivels up like a date-stalk*
> *As God ordained, who is alone the one who*
>   *wisely*
> *Contemplates this correctly, as a perfect man*
> *Understands it well, there is nothing vain about it*
> *Seek only in the Qur'an, there you will find the*
>   *plan*
> *Whoever can't find it has weak insight.*

Astrologically the zodiacal sign Cancer is the house of the moon, which represents the soul. Here the house is used for the human body. The twenty-eight stations that run the soul through the secret table of the Prophet correspond to the path of the Moon—every station is equal to the time span in which a formula is exercised. Thus the first station is the two-day exercise of *alam,* the second station likewise the three-day exercise of *alam,* the third station the seven-day exercise of *alamas,* and so forth.*

This is the path the dervish order is accustomed to taking. This not only has to do with a general sort of knowledge, but they also attempt to acquire special powers by means of a special practice. However, for the most part the dervishes are people who strive after higher knowledge, and from whom the spiritual leaders of Islam will be drawn.

If they pass the time of testing, which usually lasts 825 days, then they will receive higher initiation, if they are capable and if they have the desire. Or, on the other hand, they receive more specialized instruction in order to attain certain magical characteristics. If they show no further capabilities they just remain in the lower grades of the order.

This higher initiation is the exercise of Freemasonry, and it is, as we will see later, the work of the alchemists and Rosicrucians.

These exercises are characterized by the use of the three signs of recognition employed by modern Freemasons: sign,

---

*The twenty-ninth station is then the completion of the path, the return of the soul to a higher stage; the house, the body has become more spiritualized.

grip, and word. However, they are not signs of recognition, not mere symbols in any case, but rather magical operations designed to induct the finer radiation of primordial power—to incorporate them into the body and thereby make the body more spiritual; to give the balance of power to the spirit over the body.

The signs are three different positions of the hand, known by the vowels that they depict.

I. The *I* sign

The right hand is in a fist and from the fist the index finger is extended straight out; the hand is put in such a position that the finger is directed straight upward into the heights so that the letter *I* is represented.

II. The *A* sign

The hand is held in such a way that all the fingers lay in a flat plane; the thumb is now extended so that it forms an angle of 90 degrees, a right angle with the line of the index finger.

III. The *O* sign

One is to bend the fingers and thumb of the angled hand in such a way that the tip of the thumb just touches the tip of the index finger. The thumb, index finger and the part of the hand between these two digits form a circle, an *O*.

The grips are performed in proximity to different parts of the body.

I. The Neck Grip

One places the angled hand on the neck in such a way that the thumb touches the right carotid artery, the index finger lies on the larynx, and the other fingers are in a flat plane with the index finger. The angled hand is withdrawn sharply with the index finger moving across the larynx until the hand is situated in a position equal in height to the right shoulder, then it is allowed to drop down.

II. The Chest Grip

This grip is performed over the chest with the angled right hand. The correct height of the grip is obtained when one places the angled right hand in the neck grip and then positions the angled left hand in such a way that the thumb just touches the little finger of the right hand. That is just the right height. The grip is so positioned that the tips of the four fingers just touch the left arm, so that the palm is lying on the left breast. The hand with the outstretched thumb is drawn over to the right until the finger tips are touching the right side of the body.

III. The Middle Grip

Present-day Masonry no longer uses this grip, which is performed somewhat lower down than the chest grip. The right position is found when one places the angled right hand in the manner of the chest grip and then again places the angled left hand in such a way that the outspread thumb just touches the little finger of the right hand.

IV. The Master, or Belly, Grip

This grip is positioned by the breadth of the angled hand lower than the middle grip. It is moved from below the navel up over the solar plexus, and thus performed in a manner similar to the previous grips.

The words have already been given in the Quranic table. Before these formulas can be used, however, one first uses the three vowels:

$$I \qquad A \qquad O$$

and later the compounds:

$$s \qquad sa \qquad so$$

I and *si* are only used in connection with the *I* sign,

A and *sa* only in connection with the *A* sign, and

O and *so* only in connection with the *O* sign.

A question is posed to anyone taking on these exercises that must be answered within a time span of three days. Whether the student must undergo further instruction or may immediately enter into the exercises depends upon the answer to this question. These exercises can last for a period of time from three to twenty-five months: this depends entirely on the student. There are actually very precise signs by which one can tell whether one can proceed, or whether one must start over from the beginning. The first condition that must be met upon beginning the exercises is patience, the second perseverance, and the third courage.

The numbers I give here represent the shortest times, which should be compared to the numbers on the table on page 123. Above all one should be on notice that the work should not be rushed. "The Devil is involved in a hurried shop," says a Turkish proverb.

The indispensable condition upon entering the exercises is faith in God; the awareness that the individual is one with God. I repeat this reminder for those who wish to begin these exercises, which in no case can cause harm to anyone who has a selfless spirit. But they may be harmful to those who undertake them with the selfish intention to delve into secrets that they are not supposed to know. In that case such persons will perform the exercises without success and will become annoyed at having spent money on such a worthless book.

The work is divided into three parts:

I.   The Preliminary Work

II. The Main Work

III. The Pursuant Work

THE PRELIMINARY WORK

One stands upright, forms the *I* sign and concentrates his whole attention on the uplifted finger while continuing to think of nothing other than, *I-I-I*. One will soon notice that the finger begins to become warm in a most peculiar fashion. When this warming becomes noticeable, one allows the hand to fall and after a while the *A* sign is formed. One should attempt to vivify the *A* in a similar way until one feels a dry warmth in the thumb.

Then one immediately forms the *O* and animates it in the same way. The Oriental, who sequesters himself in the solitude of his *târiqa* (i.e., of a dervish establishment), will feel definite signs of the kind indicated on the first day; the Occidental, who will do the exercise for no more than about ten minutes in the morning or evening, will need a few days longer.

As soon as the warming takes place the student must form the *I* and animate the finger with *si-si-si* until the warming sensation is felt. The student then lets the hand drop and immediately forms the *A*. The angled hand is then animated with *sa-sa-sa* and after a while the hand is guided to the neck, the hand grip is made, and the inducted rarified forces of nature are thereby conducted to the neck. During this the student constantly thinks *sa-sa-sa,* then sharply removes the hand and forms the *O,* which, after being animated awhile with the syllable *so-so-so,* is moved to the solar plexus in the master grip.

This preliminary work encompasses a time span of ten days, consisting of three days of animation with the simple vowel sounds and seven days with the syllable made up of the vowel compounded with *S.*

THE MAIN WORK

This work is performed daily for five to ten minutes. Repeat the indicated exercises of the preliminary work for seven days. After the sixth day move the index finger of your angled hand, after it has been animated by *sa,* to your nose. If you smell a slight sulfurous odor, you can proceed. If such is not the case, you must exercise for seven days longer.

This work is performed ten minutes daily for fourteen days. The *I* is formed and animated by *si-si-si*. When warmth is felt the hand is dropped and the *A* is formed, animated by the formula *alam*. The hand is moved into the neck grip at the neck, while constantly repeating the formula. After a while remove the hand sharply. Then the *O* is formed again as before. After fourteen days the bitter taste of mercuric chloride will be perceived if the index finger of the angled hand is placed on the tongue.

The following work is performed ten minutes daily for fourteen days. The student forms the *I* sign, which is animated with *si,* then the *A* sign, which is animated with:

> two days *alam*
> two days *alamas*
> seven days *alar*
> three days *alamar*

After the first four days there will be a perceptible salty taste when one puts the index finger of the angled hand on the tongue. Then it is time to sharpen one's vision. If the student perceives a black shadow, this part of the work is finished.

Concerning the next phase of work, the table of the Prophet indicates a time span of 696 days. Depending on the individuals involved, it fluctuates between this maximum term and the minimum of three lunar months. On page 123 I compare the data of the *Rosarius minor* table with that of the Prophet. No exact time span can be set, it all depends on obtaining certain results. When these are obtained, the student goes on; otherwise the exercise is repeated until the indicated color appears. Once the student has glimpsed the blackish shadow, this day is to be celebrated as the beginning of a new life—the student receives a lodge name.

In the next period of time the chest and middle grips come into use. The student animates the *I* sign for a short while and then immediately shifts into *A,* which is animated with the indicated formula. Once one has animated the *A* sign, it is then incorporated into the body by means of the chest grip. If the color being aimed for is attained early, the other formulas are just left out and the learner goes on to the next exercise. Since the student has to report to the teacher what is seen every day, verification is easy. The formulas to be practiced during this period of work are:

alar, kaha-ya-as, taha, tasam, tas-tasam.

The colors that the student slowly begins to see are as follows: out of the blackish shadow evolves a blue, then a light red that soon fades into a pale green that becomes fresher from day to day. Once the green appears very clearly, this work is finished.

The student changes to the middle grip, with which the formulas *alam, yas, sa, cham* come into use. The developing colors show an intricate interplay and finally fade into a yellowish white. By means of the master grip and the formulas *cham, cham-asak, ka* this yellowish white is transformed into a brilliant white, which the mystics of the Orient cannot praise enough.

THE PURSUANT WORK . . .

shall turn the white of the main work into a magnificent red. The table of the Prophet indicates that the only formula for this is short *na*. This grip is called the closing grip by the masters because it is used at the end of the whole working session. It is begun to the left of the navel and is then drawn back over the navel. The white fades into a dirty gray, then it becomes yellow for a short time before developing into a full red.

With this the work of the Oriental Mason is finished— the work upon oneself. A raw, uneven stone has become a cubical one.

This curriculum is not to be interrupted. The student may not leave out a single day. Most of the Oriental Masons have only progressed through the lesser work, at the conclusion of which the signs of recognition are communicated.

These consist of certain words and signs. Hand grips are not known to them because Orientals do not greet each other by offering their hands. If one suspects that another might be a brother Mason then one makes the *I* sign by extending one's index finger horizontally so that the other one sees it: the second one responds by spreading out the thumb of the right hand. It is demonstrated that both have proven themselves to each other when they both form the circle, the *O*.

If you find a candle, a round bowl, and an open compass on the table of an Oriental person you can be certain that you are in the presence of an initiate.

If an Oriental Mason wants the aid and counsel of a brother in a social situation where no one is known, the Mason will find a brother by placing the angled right hand nonchalantly over the left shoulder, approximately where the chest grip starts. If one is in great distress, the angled hand will be lifted over the head; often also lifting both arms up and holding out both hands. It is a duty to rush at once to the aid of a brother who gives this sign.

Another sign of recognition is the so-called fire sign, which is made when one wishes to greet a brother from a distance. One holds the left hand stretched out flat, lays the right hand on it, likewise flat, and now moves the right hand quickly and energetically along the back of the left hand.

The so-called star sign, which is made in the lodge, is formed with the right hand by holding the two middle fingers together, spreading apart the small and index fingers, and spreading the thumb out as well.

The words of recognition are: key, water, fire, level, black, white, red, rose, stone. As will be understood later, these words describe the entire work. Among the Oriental Masons the work is called the science of the key, *Ilm el miftach,* and the Masons themselves often refer to themselves as sons of the key, *Beni el Mim.*

At meetings the oldest sheikh presides and a warden, a steward, and a runner are appointed. The warden has to ensure that the meeting is conducted undisturbed; the steward takes care of the guests, supervises the servants, and at the conclusion of the gathering collects an offering that is divided between the warden and the servants. The runner supports the warden and the steward.

The sheikh opens the session with the fire sign and the word *alam,* which the Beni el Mim actually use to indicate: "Let's begin." After the questions to the warden, the steward, and the runner as to whether everything is in order, the sheikh says: "My brothers, we are secure, we are provided for, and we are served. The sun is shining, let us open heaven. Brother runner, hast thou the key?"

"Worthy master, I am the *I*."

"Brother warden, hast thou the key?"

"Worthy master, I am the *A*."

"Brother steward, hast thou the key?"

"Worthy master, I am the *O*."

"My brothers, without the key there is no knowledge. I am water, fire, and level. What are you?"

The warden answers: "We are black, white, red, rose, and stone."

Then the master: "Holy is our science. Let us acknowledge: there is no God but God and Muhammad is the messenger of God." Now everyone present makes the star sign on their chests, whereupon the confession of faith is repeated simultaneously by all.

Then the presiding member goes on: "God bless him and give him salvation. Hear the words of the holy sura: In the name of God the most merciful, the gracious. *Cham osak.* Therefore God the powerful, the wise, gives his revelation to you and those who were before you."

The master recites the 42nd sura and concludes with the words: "True are the words of the Prophet, God bless him and give him salvation. Brother warden, what are the sun and moon?"

"Allah wad din." That means: "God and soul or also religion and faith." *Din* is ambiguous, and so the question is one of the main questions of the brotherhood.

All those present repeat the answer of the warden and thereby complete the star sign.

The master goes on: "To worship God and to make the faith great, is always our effort."

All present answer with *"alam,"* and now the subject of the evening is entered upon. After the conclusion of the official segment, a convivial meal usually takes place.

The greatest discretion is required of the Beni el Mim. However, in order to forestall the idea that the present book is any sort of betrayal, it must be said that it has been written by command of the chiefs of the order. The reason is as follows: the so-called civilized world has been overcome by a great organization of infidels—monstrous in extent—and religious institutions have already been undermined by this to such a degree that they are not able to mount any unified resistance. In this emergency the Islamic brothers remembered that the tradition says that in earlier times the science was known in Europe. They sought and investigated—and found—in the writings of the Rosicrucians and the alchemists that these exemplified the science of the key perfectly. The assignment is to make people aware of this and to show seekers the way: the requirements of the times cause any consideration against publication to vanish. May the truth of the process of victory begin and the clouds of darkness slowly, but all the more surely, disperse.

"Alam."

SUMMARY OF THE WORK

Preparation

Animation of the signs *I, A, O* through the vowels *I, A, O*

Animation of the signs through *si, sa, so*

Main work

Neck grip using formulas: *alam, alamas, alar, alamar*

Chest grip using formulas: *alar, kaha-ya, taha, tasam, tas, tasam*

Middle grip using formulas: *alam, yas, sa, cham*

Stomach grip using formulas: *cham, cham, asak, ka*

Pursuant Work

Closing grip using formula: *na*

Theory

So far we have been introduced to the practice of Islamic Freemasonry, now we must present evidence to show that the science of the key is actually the preparation of the philosopher's stone, the *magnum opus,* the mystery of the Rosicrucians and alchemists.

Anyone knowledgeable about these writings will recognize the connections with ease, if they are not so stupid as to think that such a recognition is detrimental—that is, the dogma or opinion that one already knows everything. I do not undertake to oppose such an opinion, for that would be a useless beginning. I console myself with a verse I once read somewhere:

The philosopher Pythagoras conceived
A new doctrine, and so he brought—

Since he was, of course, still a heathen—
A thousand sacrificial bulls to the Gods.
Is it now no wonder, if the oxen tremble
As soon as they get wind of a new truth?

What I am revealing here is old, primeval knowledge. I cannot be credited with having discovered the secret; I am only the means to an end, the tool. And this tool has struggled long enough against revealing this secret. It was supposed to be revealed only to a small circle in my *Die Geschichte der Astrologie* (History of Astrology); I confess that was a conceit of mine.

For those who are not familiar with the mode of teaching and symbolism of the Rosicrucians, I will give the necessary explanations. Additionally, there are enough books in the Theosophical Publishing House where more detailed information can be found. It is likewise with the symbols and signs of recognition of the Freemasons. Modern Freemasonry has truly preserved one thing and that is that a great portion of the symbols are still used in the lodges, even though the meaning might have been lost or another external meaning might have been applied. I once presented this years ago in magical writings under the pseudonym Lessing the Younger (*Conversations Ernst and Falk*).

Modern Freemasonry, which since the Constitution of

1717 was developed into worldwide Freemasonry, both *is* and *is not* the continuation of the old Freemasonry of the Middle Ages. It is so far as outward appearances are concerned, but as concerns the nature and content of the teaching it has entirely abandoned the ways of ancient Masonry. It has placed itself on a purely humanistic basis and views salvation as a matter of external progress moving from the outside inward. Ancient Masonry views, or rather viewed, its assignment as the ennobling of the individual. It taught a system whereby the individual being had to begin to become better, and it hoped that this person would then function like leavening in the mass of the people. This hope was justified as long as there remained a religious unity in the Western world. As soon as this unity began to crumble, the powers of the shadow started to win the game and the emerging Enlightenment gradually overwhelmed the old sources completely such that the meanings of the symbols were forgotten.

Modern Masonry has no system of exercises such as ancient Masonry did. The word *Jachin,* which is imparted to the apprentice, signifies nothing to him other than it is a sign of recognition of the 1st-degree. However, that the two vowels *I* and *A* are contained in this word, and that these are the work of the 1st-degree, has been forgotten. The column Jachin is the upward pointing index finger, just as still today all minarets around the mosques are compared to index fingers.

The column Boas is the thumb. In the 2nd-degree the apprentice is to work on the *A* and the *O*. He is to go from the point to the line (*I*), from the line through the compass (*A*) to a perfect circle (*O*). This is the meaning of the letter *G*, which means geometry, of the Masonic 2nd-degree.

And what does the 3rd-degree mean to the present-day Mason? This apprentice receives the master word and the master grip, but does not know that the word must be made true by means of the grip, so that out of the discolored ashes the full redness of the rose can be engendered. Only through the black shadow of death can the spirit attain its complete unfoldment.

It is telling enough that most historians of Freemasonry reject Rosicrucianism and alchemy as aberrations; but no, it was precisely these that embodied ancient Freemasonry. If we trace our way back we will find significant connections. In my second volume of *Die Geschichte der Astrologie* I will pursue these connections. It is there that one also finds the basis of the teachings concerning letters and numbers, which I can only touch on here.

We will become familiar with numerous alchemical and Rosicrucian writers in the following presentation. I am concerned with demonstrating from these writings the proof that the exercises of the Beni el Mim embody the great work, which the Rosicrucians and alchemists have described as the highest of all. I want to open the way to the understanding of these things so that even the doubter can enter upon it. Without doubt, further investigations by those more suitable than I will increase the proofs, but I know that for many this will not be necessary.

It is ancient, secret knowledge that everything in the world—that the whole universe—consists of a primeval substance, and that matter as we know it is only an apparent form of this primeval matter. The ancients called this primeval matter *aether* (ether), and they taught that God, the ultimate, incomprehensible unity, is manifested as spirit and ether. Modern science expresses this by saying that every form of matter is determined by a different vibratory rate of the primeval substance. Even just twenty years ago it was taught that the atom was the smallest thing and was indivisible; today it is taught that in the atom a certain number of electrons circulate around a fixed nucleus. The direction of motion and number of these electrons determine the nature of the matter.*

To know the nature of this primeval substance is conceptually impossible for us, but its first apparent forms are recognizable. These are cosmic forces designated by the ancients

*[Theosophisches Verlagshaus, Leipzig (Refers to C. W. Leadbeater and A. Besant, *Okkulte Chemie* [Occult chemistry]. Leipzig: Theosophical Publishing House, 1924.) —*Trans.*]

as elements: fire, water, air, and earth. By means of these the seven forces that play a role in astrology are fixed.

God (Sun) is manifest in the spirit (Moon) and matter/ether (Saturn). Spirit and matter are manifest in the four cosmic forces: fire (Mars), earth (Venus), air (Mercury), and water (Jupiter). In astrology a zodiacal sign is ascribed to each of these forces as a diurnal and nocturnal house. The sequence of zodiacal signs as nocturnal houses represents the materialization of spirit, while the sequence of the diurnal houses represents the spiritualization of matter.

SUN		MOON
Leo		Cancer
Virgo	Mercury	Gemini
Libra	Venus	Taurus
Scorpio	Mars	Aries
Sagittarius	Jupiter	Pisces
Capricorn	Saturn	Aquarius

Here the goal of human development is presented in this ordering of the zodiacal signs in the simplest and most comprehensible form. Each person must undergo this development; however, the free will of the human being makes it possible to accelerate this development. One way to spiritualize matter is the science of the key.

I is the creative principle, the first unity. From the *I* arises the *A,* spirit, and the *O,* matter. By means of the three vowels, spiritual currents are stimulated. We very frequently find these two signs, and *A,* represented in images in ancient Freemasonic literature, and less frequently the *O.*

Two very good illustrations of the vowels are found in the 1619 Hannover edition of Heinrich Khunrath's *Amphitheatrum Sapientiae Aeternae.* Khunrath was a physician in Dresden. Although the work did not appear until three years after Khunrath's death, he had already secured imperial permission to publish the book from the then mint master of the elector by the name of Sebottendorff in 1598. His lodge brother Erasmus Wolfart provided for the publication. The three vowels are found on the first table, which shows two crossed torches in the middle: the *A.* Over these is an owl, as a symbol of wisdom. The owl is wearing glasses: the *O.* To the right and left are two lights, which indicate the *I.* The inscription below reads:

> *What's the use of torches, light, or glasses*
> *If the people don't want to see?*

Khunrath indicates the way in the following words: "Consider why you have come into the world: to learn to know God, yourself, and the spiritual world." You arrive at this:

I. Through prayer in the oratory

II. Through work in the laboratory

That is the highest philosophy.

An illustration that shows us how the vowels are represented by the hands is found on another page of the same work.

The fourth table illustrates two wise men in the foreground who are showing the crowd the entrances to art. The wise man to the left is clearly forming an *I*, the one to the right forms an *A* with his right hand and an *O* with his left. An epigram makes the symbols even more clear; it says: *Capiat et sapiat qui capere et sapere potest, qui non vel taceat vel discat aut abeat aut talis, qualis est, maneat.* "Grasp and use it, whosoever can grasp and use it, whosoever cannot do so, be silent and learn, or remove himself, or remain as he is."

In the holdings of the Munich Staatsbibliotek there is a prayer book of the French Freemason Jacques Coeur, which is especially instructive, that contains copious illustrations of the three vowels. Franz Boll presented a study of this prayer book in 1902.*

Jacques Coeur was a merchant from Bourges who was

Zeitschrift für Bücherfreunde Vol. VI: 2 (1902)

often in Damascus, and who perhaps learned the science of the key there. He supported the campaign of Joan of Arc, was the advisor of King Charles VII, and died in 1456 on the island of Chios. His two houses in Montpellier and Bourges are famous in the context of cultural history as we find in both a number of Freemasonic emblems and epigrams. The house in Bourges is set off with two towers, one of which portrays an index finger, the other a thumb.

In the vestibule of the cathedral in Freiburg are figures whose hand positions are especially instructive. The series is derived from Albertus Magnus who makes us aware of the entire system of ancient Freemasonry by means of descriptions of the same things in his *Mineralium libri quinque*. For example, he describes the form of the *A* as follows: *Cassiope est Virgo sedens in Cathedra habens manus erectas et cancellatas.* "Cassiopeia is a Virgin, sitting in an armchair with her hands uplifted and crossed."* From the sentences that follow, it then becomes clear that the *A* is only made with the right hand. Much information is made available in the books of Louis Herre concerning the vestibule cycle of sculptures and the Masonic interpretation of the Freiburg cathedral. This literature is easy to obtain.

From the plethora of material, I wish to present another

---

*Opera omnia Parisiis, Vol V (1890), *Lib* II Tract III, Chap. V, page 54

two examples, which are especially instructive; they demonstrate the way in which the wise concealed their wisdom.

In the book *von dem großen Stein der uralten daran so viel tausend Meister anfangs der Welt hero gemacht haben,** published for the benefit of the sons of philosophy by Johannes Thölden, Hessen, Zerbst 1602—the author gives us a clue by means of a riddle from the tractate of the Benedictine Basilius Valentinus (ca. 1550). It goes like this: for a final departure from here you should, of all things, understand that you should weigh on the heavenly scale—ram, bull, crab, scorpion, and mountain goat. On the other side of the scale, however, you should put the twin, archer, water bearer, fish, and maiden. Then make sure that the gold-rich lion enters the womb of the virgin, so that the balance will be tipped to that side of the scale. Then let the twelve signs of heaven come into opposition with the Pleiades, thus a final conjunction and connection of all the colors of the cosmos will occur so that the greatest will become the least and the least will become the greatest of all.

We write the Latin names of the zodiacal signs in the usual way one under the other and read the final letters:

---

*[Concerning the great stone of the ancients, which so many thousands of masters have heroically pursued from the beginning of the world —*Trans.*]

Libra		Gemini	
Caper	ars	Arcitenens	is
Taurus		Amphora	
Cancer		Pisces	as
Scorpio	ros	Vir-Leo-go	
Aries		Pleiades	os

The solution results in *ars ros is as os*. Art is a *tau** [= dew] from *is, as* or the art of the rose is *is, as, os*.

We find the second proof in the secret figures of the Rosicrucians, which were reprinted in German translation in Altona in 1785. I do not recall whether it is contained in the reprint issued by Barsdorf (Berlin, 1918), the first part of which is *Aureum seculum redivivum von Henricus Madathanus, theosophus, medicus et tandem dei gratia aureae crucis frater.*[†] Madathan says: "The number of my name is MDCXI, in which my whole name has been written secretly in the book of nature with 11 dead and 7 living things. Additionally, the fifth letter is the fifth part of the eighth and the fifth part of the twelfth. Let yourself be satisfied with this."

The name HENRICVS MADATHANVS consists of

---

*[*Tau* means "dew" in German. Dew is a kind of alchemical distillation in nature. —*Trans.*]

†[The Golden Age renewed by Heinrich Madathan—theosopher, physician, and finally by the grace of God, a brother of the golden cross. —*Trans.*]

eleven consonants and seven vowels. If the letters that can also stand for Roman numerals are read the date 1611 results.* The fifth letter is *I*, the eighth *S*, the twelfth *A*. If we write the *S* in an angular manner thus ⊐ then *I* is the fifth part of *S* and the fifth part of *A*, which with its crossbar actually consists of five parts. So Madathan also gives us the two vowels *I* and *A*, and the consonant *S*—*is* and *as*—as guideposts.

The Masonic neck grip is found very frequently in old sculptures; a reproduction is given by Guido von List in his *Bilderschrift der Ario-Germanen*. Besides this it is also addressed by Louis Herre in his books on the Freiburg cathedral.

In alchemistic literature this neck grip is referred to as the seal of Hermes, or merely as the seal, or the bath of Mary. The Venetian physician Laurentius Ventura writes:† *Stude ergo ad inveniendum hoc sigillum secretum: quia sine illo magisterium perfici non potest, et hoc est duplex modus: primus per torturam colli*, that is: ". . . therefore concern yourself with finding this secret seal, because without that mastery cannot be attained. And there is a doubled method of practice: the first is by means of encircling‡ the neck."

---

*[These letters would be, when put in order: ICVMDV (1-100-5-1000-500-5 added together equals 1611) —*Trans.*]

†*De Lapide Philosophorum* ch. XVII printed in the *Theatrum Chemicum*, Strassburg.

‡[Sebottendorff translates as *durch Pressen:* "by means of pressing." —*Trans.*]

On the seventh page of the previously mentioned work by Basilius Valentinus we find a man who is holding a scale in his left hand, and the right hand encompasses a bottle with the neck grip. The level of importance the translator Thölde places on this drawing can be seen in his polemic that he directed at a greedy reprinter of his book, who had incorrectly reproduced the drawings. The distorted drawings are also found in the Strassburg editions of 1645 and 1666. Concerning the seal, or the bath of Mary—the expression comes from the Alexandrian alchemist, Maria Phrophetissa— Arnold of Villanova writes:* *item nota, quod ignis primi gradus qui pertinet solum ad putrefactionem, solutionem, mortificationem corporis, dicitur per quandam similitudinem balneum, quia balneum est res temperata, non intensa in calore nec etiam rigida sed calure remisso*—"Likewise notice that the degree of the first fire, which only extends to the putrefaction, dissolution, and mortification of the body, is said to be the result of a certain bath of similarity, because the bath is a moderate thing, neither harsh in its warmth, nor cold, but rather relaxed in its warmth."

Before I go on to a discussion of the work itself, I want to quote yet another passage, which I take from a book of a now unknown author. It is the *Liber de Magni Lapidis Compositione et Operatione*. The small work is made up of

---

*De Decoctione Lapidis Philosophorum

fifty-six short chapters and is found in the collection of Freemasonic writings that the Italian physician Guielmus Gratrolus of Bergamo compiled and published in Basel in 1561. The title of this collection is *Verae Alchemiae Metallicae Doctrina Certusque Modus.*

Cap. XXXV
Primum opus:
Elixir ubique reperiri

Item de vera compositione Elixiris, quod est primus opus, dicitur a philosophis quod illa res quae est vera, ubique reperitur, quia in quodlibet homine est et apudquemlibet hominem reperitur: et Adam secum apportavit eam de Paradiso et cum mortuus fuit, ipsam secum reportavit et com ea sepultus fuit: Et pro tanto dicit sapientum Allegoria, quod ist res est sol subtiliatus is est arum subtiliatum et conversum in virtute maxima minerali: unde dicitur in libro de hoc auro, ex gumma nostra et pauco auro multa emimus. Sed secundum Albertum in libro de Mineralibus dicitur et probatur, quod aurum ubiqueest et reperitur, quia non est aliqua res ex quatuor elementis elementata, in qua non inveniatur aurum in ultima affinatione naturaliter. Et quia idem Albertus dicit ibidem et probat, quod maxima virtus mineralis est in quodlibet homine et maxime in capite inter dentes ita quod in sepulchris antiquorum mortuorum inter dentes aurum in granis minutis et oblongis suerius inventum est in suo tempore, ut ipse dicit, quod esse non posset,

nisi in homine esset ista virtus mineralis, quae virtus mineralis

est in Elixiri nostro praedicto, vel composito. Et pro tanto dici-

tur quod hic lapis est in quodlibet homine et quod, Adam, etc.

His visis et intellectis ad propositum redeamus.

In the future I will not provide the Latin texts, but will limit myself to their translations.

Chapter 35
First Work:
The Elixir Is to Be Found Everywhere

Likewise the philosophers tell of the composition of the elixir, which is the first work that is that thing, which is right and found everywhere, because it is in every person and is found with every person. Adam took it with him from paradise, he bore it back when he died, and he was buried with it. For this reason the allegory of the wise says that this thing is the rarified sun, that is rarified gold brought to the highest power of the mineral. Therefore it is said in a book about this gold: we buy much from our gum and from little gold. According to Albertus in a book about minerals it is said and proven that gold is present, and can be found everywhere because there is nothing made of the four elements that does not quite naturally contain gold in the most extreme purity. Therefore he

also says that it is found everywhere. The same Albertus
says and proves right there that the greatest mineral power
is in every person and mainly in the head between the
teeth, so that in his time gold was found in the graves of
long-dead persons between their teeth on the surface in fine
elongated kernels, which, as he says, would not be possible
if that mineral power were not in the person, a power that
is also in the elixir or composition we mentioned. For this
reason it is said that this stone is in every person, and that,
Adam, etc. After we have seen and understand this, we go
back to our subject.

We shouldn't think badly of a modern person if he shakes
his head over such utterances and puts this book aside. It is
meant even less for the curious—it will confuse him as well
as the superficial individual. The old philosopher quotes an
old book: the allegory of the wise, and wishes thereby to convey that the expression *gold* is to be understood according
to the way the wise understood it. He quotes Albertus, but
incorrectly in fact. Whoever does not take the trouble to read
closely will go down the wrong path.

The gold between the teeth is the word out of which,
according to the Gospel of John, everything was created. The
kernels of gold (syllables) are *minutis* and *oblongis*—"pointed"
and "broad lengthwise." *I* and *A,* which animate the body

(gum), the little gold that is necessary is rarified solar power.

Artefius teaches us in his *Clavis Majoris Sapientiae* the art *"facere descendere spiritum"** and provides the following forms in which the spirit willingly overflows: *I V X O* and *L*. Here we have the *I* and the *O; V* and *X* are two forms of the *A,* the so-called point that comes about when the thumb is not spread in a right angle and the breadth that is the right angle. The *L* means a level and a square.

We find very significant pictures in the treatise of the Italian physician Ianus Lacinius from Calabria: *Metallorum in melius mutationem Typus Methodusque* (Venice, 1546). The first illustration shows a king, who draws attention to his extended index finger—it is the beginning of the royal art. Another work is appended to this tractate, which is also very instructive: *Pretiosa mararita novella* by Petrus Bonus Ferrariensis.

Even more important for us is the short work left behind by the unfortunate Seton, and which Sendivogius published. Orthelius annotated this piece of writing: *Novum Lumen Chemicum*. Here there are twelve figures that clearly show where the way leads.

Before I go on, it should be mentioned that Seton was an adept seduced by vanity who wanted to make use of his

---

*[This translates as: "of causing to descend into the spirit." —*Trans.*]

wisdom to manufacture gold from ignoble metals. He was arrested by the Saxon Elector, Christian II, and cruelly tortured without ever betraying his secret. Sendivog freed him from prison, but unfortunately too late, as he died three months later—after he had shared out the elixir to his wife and Sendivog. Sendivogius married his widow and so came into possession of the entirety of the elixir. Afterward he passed himself off as an adept without, however, being able to produce the elixir himself. Whoever has diligently followed my discussion will already have understood that the production of the stone is only possible for someone who has mastered the science of the key. This science is, however—at least according to the notions of the world—so childish that Seton would prefer to have himself tortured and killed rather than surrender it. He wouldn't have been believed. At the conclusion I will give an example where this is made clear. If you are interested in the special field of the alchemists of the art of making gold, I recommend to you the book by Schmieder, *Geschichte der Alchemie* [History of Alchemy] (Halle, 1832). You will derive much information from it.

We find Orthelius' commentary in volume VI of the *Theatrum Chemicum* (Strassburg, 1661). This edition corresponds completely to the book I am referring to: *Novum Lumen Chymicum Michaelis Sendivogii Polni XII Figuris in Germania reperitis illustratum*, 1624.

The first figure shows the following: from the upper left a well masked hand is extended toward the bottom right. The thumb is indicated by a small elongated cloud over the top of the third hill. Only the index finger is clearly shown, the other fingers cannot be seen. There is an old saying of the Rosicrucians, which I will translate: "Whoever is not equipped with the golden rod for fishing has to take common quicksilver." By *the golden rod* they mean the angled hand— the *A*. By the expression *has to take common quicksilver,* they mean to say that he should keep his hands off.

Another drawing shows us a chemical laboratory with a furnace. The drawing is surrounded by twenty circles; of these, seven are shown on the lengthwise sides, and three are shown above and below. On the furnace there is a large diagram that should be commented upon. In the middle of the diagram a flask is shown with a small vertical mark—an *I*. Next to the furnace at the bottom is a small grate, the cover of a vent for ashes or air. The grate work has twenty-four fields—the twenty-four letters. Concerning this, Orthelius provides the commentary that the *I* is to be connected to a finger.

I wish to explain a few more of the diagrams because the diagrams of Seton are important to me precisely because the art of this adept is doubtless solid and because a man who is irreproachable in all things, Surya, could not derive anything from the *Novum Lumen Chymicum,* otherwise he would have made some comment on Schmieder's assertion.

Surya writes in volume XI of the collection *Okkulte Medizin,* "Setonius left behind only a single alchemical treatise in Latin under the title *Cosmopolitae Novum Lum chymicum.* It concerns the stone of the wise in twelve chapters, which the author may have associated in his mind with the twelve gates of Ripey." That no disclosure concerning the secret is to be expected from this work is made absolutely clear by the previously quoted oral remarks of the author. One who betrays nothing in the heat of disputation or under torture will certainly be even more circumspect at his writing desk. This treatise was published after his death by Sendivogius and appeared in different editions.

Seton knew the time had not yet come, and he paid for this knowledge with his life. In his work he clearly set down the science for those who possess the key. But the cursed hunger for gold made them all go astray.

We know that the sun represents God and the moon represents the spirit, and the soul as well, since the soul and the spirit are the same thing; the soul is the immortal spirit that struggles back toward its primeval source. The medieval Latin alphabet of twenty letters had four vowels: *A, E, I, O.* The *U* was expressed by *V.* In addition there were sixteen consonants. Based on this scholastic division, the vowel *A* was often expressed by the number seventeen. Now we see on the left side of the illustration a two-handled washtub with soil in it; on the right side the soil has disappeared and there appears something akin to the fingertips of a hand. In the sky above shine the moon and the sun. The moon is surrounded by seventeen stars, of which sixteen are quite clearly shown, while the seventeenth is indicated more faintly. Here the letters are ascribed to the first emanation of God. It should also be indicated that these letters are to be spoken aloud. The sun shows that the letters are to be fulfilled by means of divine spirit. As the accompanying text emphasizes, this only concerns the seventeenth letter, the *A*. The explanation is the following: the soil in the washtub on the left is the *Terra Adamica*, the human being. The left segment of the figure is meant to indicate that the human being is the object of alchemy. The right segment provides us with the actual means for the work—the letter *A*, the spirit, and the hand. The moon and the stars, illuminated by the sun in the sky in the upper part of the segment on the right, symbolize the spiritually animated letter *A*. The hand stretches itself down toward the *A*, ready to grasp it. The text belonging to this figure says, "The aforementioned spiritual water is taken up and both waters are blended in a single vessel and put outside under a clear, starry sky. Then the celestial rays are mixed with them. When, however, rain falls you can operate. The longer it is set out, the better it is."

The two waters are the spoken and the spiritually animated *A*. They are connected to each other in a single vessel, which is the angled hand, and put outside—that is, the hand is stretched out so that it can draw spiritual water out of the ether. The expression *under a clear, starry sky* is supposed to indicate the ether. When the hand is extended in this way so as to animate the *A* in it, etherical rays are mixed with the animated hand and they flow forth into it like rain. Once the hand is sufficiently saturated with this spiritual water, then one proceeds on to the operation—the neck grip.

The water is defined as "our heavenly water that does not wet our hands, not normal water, yet almost like rainwater."

I wish to describe one last figure. On this one we see an alchemist who is holding the *tragula aurea,* "the golden javelin," in his left hand with which he is pointing to a washtub. The tub is empty, whereby it is indicated that this has nothing to do with actual water. His right hand is making a grasping gesture. On a chair stands a smaller vessel with water, and if one carefully examines this vessel a small hand can be seen to have been drawn in.

With this I believe I have fulfilled my assignment of providing proof that the secret of the alchemists is hidden in the vowels connected to signs and grips. I will therefore conclude, as I will quote other masters later on, with the words that Leonhardt Thurneisser, the much misunderstood Freemason of Basel, directed toward his readers as a conclusion. In 1586, Thurneisser forged a union of Reformed and Lutheran lodges into one great league. The *Fama* of 1614 acknowledges him as the father of the Rosicrucians and also mentions his two dictionaries along with the writings of Paracelsus. These dictionaries were only known in lodge circles and probably only survive in a few copies. One bears the title: *Hermeneia, das ist ein Onomasticum Interpretatio oder erklerunge Leonhardt Thurneyssers zum Thurm über die frebden vnd vnbekannten Wörter in den schriften Theophrasti Paracelsi.** It is ninety-five pages long and was printed in Berlin in 1574. The last two pages contain a rhymed poem to the reader as a conclusion to the work. In this Thurneisser represents the viewpoint that Freemasonic practices will lead to better and higher knowledge than going to the greatest universities. Our hand grips, he says, reveal the truth to us much better and more clearly than any book. Also, all obscure writings will become clear by these means, and whatever we do not understand in Paracelsus will be easily understood when we connect the question to a hand grip.

---

*[*Hermeneia* that is an Onomasticum Interpretation or explanations by Leonhardt Thurneisser zum Thurm concerning foreign and unknown words in the writings of Theophrastus Paracelsus. —*Trans.*]

We inquire with the chest grip and God provides the answer
in our hearts. The concluding words read:

> *Much of Art is written 'bout, little is true,*
> *Hand-signs show the experiment, work makes it*
>   *clear.*
> *Practice confirms the things that are written,*
> *Hand-signs are the Art thus worked through.*
> *The hand-sign is an instrument*
> *By which the mind concludes all its calculations.*
> *Nature rewards the mind with its desire*
> *Once the hand-sign has done its work.*
> *But nothing at all happens without the*
>   *hand-sign—*
> *The influence functions invisibly.*
> *So that which I cannot read*
> *I grasp with my hands,*
> *And deliver my praise to God,*
> *That which a hundred couldn't do by reading,*
> *Therefore prattling envy does not concern me.*

Theory and Practice

In what has already been written I have provided proof that the system of the Rosicrucians and alchemists can only be understood when signs, grips, and words are used. We are now going to go through the whole system in light of the science of the key. Please allow me to give a few additional examples of proof from Rosicrucian writings here. The system according to which Westerners work is not completely perfect, since the middle grip, the closing grip, and a series of the formulas were not known to the West. All systems that were exercised, however, dovetail into the system of the Beni el Mim without contradiction.

The wish, and the hope, of those who assigned me the task of writing this book is that a great number of individuals will want to undertake these exercises, thus building an unbreakable chain, which is the best defense against all the powers of the shadow. To avoid any misunderstandings, I would like to stress that I reject the formation of any lodge, and I request also that I not be bothered by letters. I will not answer; as those who know me from my astrological writings can attest. What I have to say is so clear that a child can grasp it. Whoever can't understand it cannot be helped. It is written, "Seek and ye shall find"; but this does not mean that everything should be handed out on a silver platter.

The exercises can harm no one. But one condition must be met—they cannot be interrupted. Missing one day will cause a setback of weeks and call the whole endeavor into question. And the most important thing is the prayer—the prayer for admission.

The exercises, especially in the beginning, should not be overdone; otherwise a few complaints might arise. These would not be dangerous, but they would be uncomfortable. I will provide further explanations of these. You should practice when you are alone and undisturbed. Anyone can be sequestered ten minutes a day for this. You should keep quiet about your exercises and only speak about them once your goal is met—to someone you recognize as an equal brother—for then it is easy.

A question I hear asked is: what mode of life must I maintain? I would like to answer this as well. One who studies the lives of the alchemists and Rosicrucians will find that they were married and that they lived as every other person lived. True wisdom automatically avoids any excess. The Oriental generally lives modestly, consuming milk, cheese, bread, and fruit; a sheep is only slaughtered on festival days. This is perhaps not possible in the colder latitudes, but the consumption of meat should be limited in a reasonable way. Alcohol in every form is forbidden to the Muslim. Now a glass of wine or beer when you are in a happy mood won't hurt anything, but distilled liquors are strenuously warned against. Those who get to the end of the exercises will know precisely what is to be given up.

It is best to undertake the exercises early in the morning right after rising—they will not take any more than ten minutes a day. During the day, when you are alone, you can do a short repetition, and in the evening as well.

I will not give a prescription concerning said prayer. Each individual will have to settle that personally. Whosoever asks, to him shall be given according to the measure he possesses. Whoever understands this correctly knows what is meant.

We read that finer forces can be attracted by the index finger held vertically and by thinking of the letter *I*. The body of the ordinary human is an inert mass that, left to itself, will become increasingly more material. In order to be able to absorb spiritual water a breach must first be opened and matter has to be stimulated. This happens by means of the letter *I*, by which the element of fire is stimulated. As I discussed in *Geschichte der Astrologie* (vol. I), *I* is the *is* rune, which is associated with Mars (fire); the rune *ar* or *as* belongs to Jupiter (water) and the *othal* rune to Mercury (air).

In order to animate the *I* correctly one places oneself in an erect position so that the whole body is given the form of the *I*. One stretches one's arm straight up to the sky and makes a fist. Then the index finger is extended upward. It should rise up next to the closed fist like a slender minaret beside the dome of a mosque, as sheikh Jachya remarks in his small book *Charam el din*. By thinking the vowel *I* the finger is animated. Some old instructions say: take the philosophical steel (*Chalyb's* index finger) and strike the *scintilla* (sparks). Then take the second steel (the thumb) and put the magnet (the *A* sign) into action, which attracts the elements and conducts to you the water for which you thirst.

It will soon be found that the finger will start to become warm and then by an act of will this current can be conducted throughout the whole body, as can the current stimulated by the *A*. This can be done without injury, but care should be taken not to influence the head—it must remain free. Otherwise a dangerous state of intoxication could ensue. During the gradual course of the work the current would automatically make its way into the head; we consciously block entrance to the head by means of the neck grip. If we form the *A* sign and animate it, we will first take in spiritual fire, but also some of the spiritual element of earth, which can be noticed by a certain dryness at the base of the thumb. If the angled hand has been sufficiently prepared it will begin to absorb the spiritual water.

We supply spiritual air to the solar plexus by means of the *O* sign. Here I would like to mention an experiment that my teacher conducted. He ordered a student to form the *A* and to think of the *O*. After a while he cried out: "O, sheikh, look, it's impossible, they are warping automatically." "My son," Mehemed Rafi said, "you see that it is impossible to mix up the signs and the words. You can only think of the *A* in the *A* sign and not the *O*, if you think of *O*, your fingers will automatically try to close up. You see that the signs are not chosen arbitrarily, but rather are founded in nature. It is our assignment in life to seek the spirit, but we always work in harmony with nature. You also see, however, my son, that spirit acts acutely in our bodies as it forms the body according to its image. It is not only the *I*, the *A*, and the *O*, which animate the body, all vowels and consonants have this ability. The *I* spirit provides the breadth, dignity, and resilience, the *O* spirit imparts life and movement."

It was at the beginning of my study when I heard these words that sheikh Mehemed Rafi spoke to the Bektashi dervish, whom he was introducing to the *Ilm el miftach*. I was very impressed—no astrologer could have defined the effects of the planetary forces more simply.

Approximately ten days are necessary for the preparatory work. Nothing will be harmed if the simple vowels and syllables are exercised longer—development will take place faster that way. When the preparation is over, transition is made into the main work, which is the actual chemical process. In the preparatory work the spirit held in the fetters of matter is stimulated, or as the alchemists express it, the materials are made ready, the soil, the earth, is tilled in order to be able to receive the seed. By means of the limited spiritual animation of the finger, ether is absorbed and conducted to the body. The manifestations we observe are: the body breathes quite freely, and the body seems to become lighter.

As we go further in the work we will become aware that increasing warmth is developing in the index finger. Because of its form, this pointed member attracts more of the fire element—which should also be brought about by means of the vowel *I*. Finally the warmth becomes so strong that fire flames forth from the point of the finger and creates a sulfurous acridity with the air that we can clearly perceive when we hold our finger to our nose. Most old writings remark first of all on the preparation of the sulfur. Flamel writes about this: At last I found what I was looking for, which I recognized at once by its strong smell. When I had that, I easily perfected my mastery.*

This sulfurous smell is the first milestone on the path. Only one who perceives it can go further. Then the experience will be that of a current flowing into the angled hand, a flow that the ancients very pointedly compared to water. This is the water of life our folktales are so enthusiastic about, the *aqua vitae* of the alchemists. With the sulfurous smell the dissolution has begun, the *putrefactio* of alchemy. The ancient writings, in agreement with Oriental texts, fix a minimal length of forty days in which a certain result must be obtained. A few other Freemasonic texts declare, however, that it would take seventy or even ninety days to complete the first degree.

The *putrefactio,* or decay, comes to an end when the disciple of the art glimpses a blackish shadow, the raven's head of the alchemists.

During this time we are conducting the water of life into the body by means of the neck grip. This water has the characteristic of dissolving and disintegrating anything coarse. Hand in hand with this disintegrating effect goes another one that builds things up. The finer forces in the person are conditioned in such a way that they can be awakened. Ancient Freemasons very often compared the birth of the spiritual

---

*Albert Poisson, *Nikolas Flamel: Sa vie, ses fondations, ses oeuvres, suivi de la réimpression du livre des figures.* Paris (1893), p. 173.

man to physical birth. The blackish shadow the disciple sees with the spiritual eye is the evolving spiritual person. Now with the application of the neck grip, the one the ancients called the *Balneum Mariae,* care should be given to making this sign precisely. "Cut off the neck of the beast," says an old text. The grip should not be overdone, however, so that a slow annealing is the result. It can happen, and the ancient Freemasons describe this process often, that the fire element breaks out and anneals the vertebra. If this occurs do not be afraid, just bow your head and wait for the affliction to be over—the terrible flame will go out after a few minutes. If you are prepared for the manifestation you have nothing to fear. As a rule, however, this annealing occurs slowly and gradually without being noticed. If the flame breaks out it is as if a terrible demon is grabbing the person by the scruff of the neck and taking him down to the ground.

After approximately two weeks of this exercise no one will be able to doubt any longer that the neck grip has caused chemical changes in the neck. Now the time has come when the poisonous taste of mercury is perceived on the tongue whenever the tongue is touched with the index finger of the angled hand. Then later the taste of salt is developed. About this Seton says: "Therefore the fire began to affect the air and generated sulfur. For its part the air began to affect the water and generated quicksilver. Also the water began to affect the earth and generated salt." This process is described and concealed by alchemists in the most manifold ways. I do not wish to speak about the basis of the usage of the consonants, and why the vowels work in this way, that would lead us astray and make this book too bulky. If you want to be informed on this further, see my *Geschichte der Astrologie*. So, the formulas should be understood as they are intended: as means to develop the spiritual body.

When our spiritual eye glimpses the blackish shadow the purification is concluded, and now the main point becomes the unfolding of the evolving spiritual body—a work that takes varying lengths of time. The neck grip, or the bath of Mary, only works from the lower stratum out of which the spiritual person, free of the fetters of the body, should rise. The earthly body must be mortified so that the spiritual body can rise up. Here a note needs to be added. This mortification has been much misunderstood. It was believed that the body had to be killed by means of asceticism and withdrawal from the world. This is naturally only one possible path if the pilgrim has also completed a whole change in consciousness. Without this, a false mortification ensues. Asceticism and withdrawal from the world lead in most cases to a dissolution in which the pilgrim becomes easy prey for every type of evil influence. More than a few black magicians have in this way become the victims of the Prince of the Shadow.

True mortification lies in sublimation, in unification, in the *unio mystica,* in becoming one with God. The unification begins with a change in consciousness wherein the mortification of the small ego is completed and the resurrection of the divine ego takes place. That is, moreover, the goal we wish to achieve—which we must and can achieve.

Once we have arrived at the end of our exercise we will feel that our earthly bodies are becoming more and more strange, we are growing beyond them, we clearly feel they have become dust and ashes. This is the deepest point, which is reached when we are surrounded by the terrors of darkness and death. For this reason the ancient Freemasons only took courageous candidates into their community, and the tests they had to undergo were very severe. Courage and perseverance were the most noble virtues required.

Our work is aimed at anticipating and overcoming death. Usually the human soul parts from its body only upon death. We do not want such a conclusion to our lives. We want to undergo a voluntary death in the middle of our lives. The weakling will be terrified by the boldness of our undertaking. We can only conquer nature by means of nature—the lower by means of the higher, spiritual nature. We remain strictly in conformity with the spiritual and natural universe.

A person of little faith could accuse me of tempting God,

of lacking necessary humility, to which such a person volun-
tarily submits in the natural course of affairs, as we are used to
it. I answer by saying that I am pointing to a path of life that
lies in the essence of every true religion and that this way is
also clearly recognizable in the New Testament. Most modern
people unfortunately have not read the holy scriptures of their
religion. Those who have followed me to this point, but who
now recoil, are advised to read no further—for what I bring is
not milk for the weak, but food for the strong.

All religions teach the sevenfold constitution of the body.
Precise knowledge can best be obtained on this by studying
the Rosicrucian lessons of Heindel. I can only offer a brief
sketch here. The designations are of archaic origin, the translations render the approximate meanings:

The Immortal Part

   1. Atma, the self, God in us   Sun

   2. Buddhi, the heavenly soul   Moon

   3. Buddhi-Manas, reason, causal body   Mercury

The Mortal Part

   4. Kama-Manas, intellect   Venus

   5. Kama-body (astral body), desire   Mars

   6. Prana (Linga-Bhuta, etheric body), life force   Jupiter

   7. Sthula-Bhuta, body   Saturn

Apparently this table of correspondences is at variance with the version generally used in Theosophy. However, those who have worked intensively with planetary forces will recognize that this difference is not an essential one. With the addition of Uranus and Neptune these two higher octaves of Mercury and Venus are assigned to a second principle— but here we are not looking at the more developed person, rather we are only concerned with one who is just beginning to evolve. There Saturn stands at the threshold, it is assigned to the Kama-Manas, for us it is the representative of the most dense form of matter.

The last quadrad is called "the animal in us" by Paracelsus. The science of the key gives us the way to conquer this animal in us and to ascend to the causal plane. This is all the more necessary as the powers of darkness are already working to make a noose for the person who is making such progress. I can only allude to things here, but some will understand what I mean.

Many of our brothers have advanced so far that they have ascended from stage seven to the sixth stage and they are in a position to project the fluid body, whose vessel is the life force, thus splitting themselves in two. The phenomenon of the double (*Doppelgänger*) can be traced back to this ability— as can many other spiritualistic phenomena and occult experiences. Now during the projection of the fluid body, it remains connected to the earthly body by means of a cord. However, this connection is very loose. This is the point of attack where the powers of the shadow will strike; where they must strike.

For this reason it is most important that the possibility of leaving the plane of effects to gaze upon the causal plane is provided—this is what my teachers desire. Every danger loses its terror as soon as it is understood. But we will not cease our work. We press forward through death toward true life. The body will also appear to us as dust and ashes when we are finished with the work of the neck grip. Thus the writings of the ancient Freemasons warn us: *cinerem ne vilipendas*.* We regard the ashes, the body, with great care, for we need it for the construction of the new, spiritual body. It is not enough that we have developed the shadow of the spiritual body—we must give it color, form, and thus an independent life.

AFTER DEATH—LIFE

For the development of the spiritual body we employ the other grips and, in addition, use the formulas of the Prophet. Before I go on I would like to quote a passage from the previously cited Flamel: "And truly, I say to you once more, even if you work with the correct materials, if, at the beginning, after

---

*["You are not to hold ash in slight regard." —*Trans.*]

you have put the mixtures into the philosophical egg—that is, a while after the fire has acted upon it—you do not see this raven's head, this deep-black blackness, you must start all over again." The philosophical egg is the body; the mixtures are the fine mixtures of the elements which we conducted to the body by means of the neck grip. Therefore it is of the greatest importance that this shadow is seen. If it appears, you are on the right track. This raven's head is mentioned by all alchemists and writers, and the colors that start to appear are correspondingly described by all. The main colors are: black, white, red. Between white and red there are a number of other colors—especially a citrine color. The spiritual body is developed in these colors, the natural order of which can be disturbed by a fire that is too strong—or as we like to express it—by an excessive frequency of the use of the chest grip. This grip should not be made more than five times a day. Even if the old texts say "Boil, boil unceasingly," they mean by this that one should not lose patience. Here I will collate the table of *Rosarius minor* and the table of the Prophet so that the apprentice will have reference points for the time periods for the exercises. But first is the translation of this old text that demonstrates the process of the work most clearly.

And this alone I reveal: Through such a regime you will have completed the purification in 124 days. Blackness is, however, the recognized sign of purification. Furthermore, you will, by means of the aforesaid regime, have a second sign—which will be a redness—that abides for thirty days and develops completely in these days. The third sign is, however, a green that is completed in seventy days by means of warmth. Between the third and fourth signs, all colors that can be conceived of will appear. Then the marriage will be consummated—the union and blending of spirit and soul, for then the two will rule together, while previously each ruled for itself under its own sign. Actually in the first sign the body ruled, in the second the spirit, and in the third the soul. The time of blending will be completed during a regularly increasing regime of seventy days. Now the fourth sign will appear, which is the profitable Azymation—140 days will go by and then the sign of whiteness will be seen.

Work	Rosarius Minor	Table of the Prophet
Preparation	14 days	46 days
Neck grip	124 days	58 days
Chest grip	100 days	149 days
Middle grip	70 days	236 days
Master grip	140 days	311 days
Closing grip	28 days	68 days
Total Days	476 days	868 days
Lunar months	17 months	31 months

It can be seen that the differences are considerable, and they are even greater in reality, because it depends entirely upon the talent of the individual—what one accomplishes in a week will take another a month, or several months. There are disciples graced by God who have completed the path in three months.

Ancient Freemasons called the chest grip the cooking. While the neck grip develops a gentle warmth, the chest grip causes the unfolding of a powerful fire. With this grip the following will be experienced: after the angled hand is animated by the formula, the spiritual water is absorbed, a fist is made and the thumb of the closed hand is placed upon the left side of the chest. Now the hand is angled and opened and the chest grip is performed and drawn off. The colors that show themselves during this operation develop from a light blue, through red to green. This red was called by the alchemists the false red, the false redness in contrast to the purple color during the closing work. If they saw the green they would cry: *"O benedicta viriditas."**

Since melted gold appears to have a green shimmer, the opinion of people who see the alchemical process as the art of making gold was once more led astray by this. The joyous cry had nothing to do with gold, but rather the Freemason was

---

*["O blessed green color" (by association, "vigor") —Trans.]

happy to have glimpsed the sign that proved to him that he was on the right-path.

The green color becomes fresher day by day, and when it has become like the green of a meadow in spring this part of the work can be broken off and the rest of the work continued with.

You are now to make the transition to the middle grip with its corresponding formulas. The procedure is the same as with the chest grip. The colors that develop present a true symphony of colors. Blue, yellow, red are represented in every shade. The ancients characterized this play of color as a peacock's tail. By and by the colors fade and by the end of the work a yellowish white remains.

The grip should not be done more than five times a day. It is better to do it only three times, as too much can endanger the whole work. It should be repeated that it is impossible to speed things up with more intensive work.

> *Patience is desirable at work*
> *A quiet spirit is busy for years,*
> *Only time makes the fine bevel strong.*

At this point I would like to discuss the *chakras* briefly. The word comes from Sanskrit and means "wheel" (*chakram*, plural *chakrani*). Jung Stilling characterizes them as small flames because they are in constant flaming motion. The ancient Freemasons called them by the names of the seven planets. If they used this terminology for other things as well this only *seems* to be a contradiction. As I indicated for the constitution of mankind, so too can individual constitutions be accordingly designated by the planets. Their relationship to each other is described by Abbot Johannes Tritheim.* In the texts we usually find the following schema, which is inscribed in concentric circles. I am representing it in another form, because I wish to avoid symbols.

Saturn	Pineal gland
Jupiter	Forehead
Mars	Thyroid
Sun	Heart
Venus	Pit of the stomach
Mercury	Navel
Moon	Sexual parts

The Sun is in the middle of the concentric circles, Saturn above, the Moon below.

These *chakras,* or little flames, are nothing other than the organs of the spiritual body. The Benedictine Basilius

---

**Tractatus chemicus* in volume IV of the *Theatrum chemicum*

Valentinus speaks of them in the following words: "the king wandered through six cities in the heavenly firmament, but in the seventh he beheld his seat." Here too the investigations of Staudenmayer should be mentioned. In his book, *Die Magie als experimentale Wissenschaft,* he proves that various nerve bundles can be specially stimulated and special effects produced. We conduct spiritual forces to these easily stimulated places and thus build the spiritual body.

Once the yellowish white is obtained, you transform this into a brilliant white by means of the master grip and the correct formulas.

I close with the words of Heinrich Khunrath: "With my own eyes I saw the gold—not the common kind but that of the philosophers—with my hands I touched it, with my tongue I tasted it, with my nose I smelled it. How wondrous is God in his works."

Conclusion

I have said everything that is to be said. We must only further discuss the pronunciation of the Arabic words. They are to be pronounced as they are written, the transcription is very precise. The *S* is pronounced like a *Z,* as is the *Z* also. So one does not say *natzim* but rather *nazim.* With words of more than one syllable the emphasis is on the second syllable, *alam—alám.* The *CH* is a guttural that may cause some difficulties. It is harder than the *ch* in German *ach,* and tends more toward the *K* sound.

In Arabic the science of the key is also called the science of the scale: *Ilm el Nazan.* One also finds *Ilm el Quimiya,* the science of chemistry. This is extremely ancient material. Around 900 AD we find it in Venice, where the cornerstone of Freemasonry was laid when the science assimilated the

Syrian legend of Hiram Abif and linked the individual grades to the construction of the Temple of Solomon—and thus the science became a monopoly of the lodge.

The ancient Freemasons never thought of looking at it like that, as by that time the alchemistic books were too widely disseminated. They placed great weight on secrecy, however, because it was feared that by giving up the secret they would expose themselves to the mockery of the people. Now people can mock!

From an old treatise of the Austrian Freemason Lampspring, who lived around the middle of the fourteenth century, these words are given, which I had promised:

> *If you understand me right and well*
> *Then you will be free of error,*
> *Nothing is more important than this one thing,*
> *In which everything else is concealed.*
> *Therefore do not turn your mind away.*
> *Cooking, time, and patience are necessary,*
> *If you wish to pick the most noble fruit.*
> *Time and work should not displease you*
> *For seed and metal may only be cooked*
> *constantly and moderately,*
> *From day to day, and perhaps all week long,*
> *Then you will, in this unpretentious thing,*

Find and perfect the whole work of philosophy,

Which certainly appears impossible to most men,

Because it concerns such a simple and easy
   work—

If we showed and made it known to others

Certainly we would be mocked by men, women,
   and children

So be discreet and silent

Then you will live in peace and be without
   trouble

Not only with your neighbor, but also with God

Who gives the art and wishes to know it secretly.

Alchemy is traced back to Hermes Trismegistus—one of his sayings is given in conclusion, and with it the explanation that a modern researcher gives:

If you do not take the corporeal condition from bodies, and if you do not reformulate the non-corporeal substances into bodies, you will not obtain what you expect. If you have read this book to its conclusion you will know what is meant by this—and how Berthelot was mistaken when he explained: "If one does not remove the metallic condition from metals and if one does not extract metals from nonmetallic materials, the transmutation of metals will not succeed."

Notes

CHAPTER 1. THE LIFE OF RUDOLF VON SEBOTTENDORFF

1. For more information on Theodor Fritsch, see Goodrick-Clarke, *The Occult Roots of Nazism,* 123–28.

2. A historical description of the Germanen-Order is provided in Goodrick-Clarke, *The Occult Roots of Nazism,* 123–34.

3. See *The American Heritage Dictionary* (1975), s.v. "wanderlust."

4. The whole topic of nineteenth- and early-twentieth-century *Germanentum,* especially in esoteric circles, is discussed by Goodrick-Clarke, *The Occult Roots of Nazism.*

CHAPTER 2. THE BEKTASHI SECT OF SUFISM

1. Arberry, *Sufism,* 31–44.

2. Al-Halâj is discussed by Flowers, *Lords of the Left-Hand Path,* 122, 127.

3. Concerning the rift between orthodoxy and Sufism and for a more contextual look at the place of Sufism in the history of religion, see Eliade, *History of Religious Ideas,* 3:62–84, 113–51.

CHAPTER 3. THE MYSTERIES OF THE ARABIC LETTERS

1. Logan, *The Alphabet Effect,* 21.
2. For a representation of this chart, see Burckhardt, *Mystical Astrology According to Ibn ʿArabi,* 32–33.
3. Ali, trans. *The Holy Quran,* 2nd ed., 602.

CHAPTER 4. ALCHEMY AND SUFISM

1. For a basic discussion of this concept, see Burckhardt, *Alchemy,* 17–21.
2. For a discussion of these medieval influences of Sufism on Christendom, see Shah, *The Sufis,* 232–80.
3. See Eliade, *Yoga,* 274–92.

Bibliography

Ali, A. Yusuf, trans. *The Holy Quran.* 2nd ed. N.p.: The Muslim Students' Association, 1977.

American Heritage Dictionary, New York: Houghton Mifflin, 1975.

Arberry, Arthur John. *Sufism: An Account of the Mystics of Islam.* New York: Harper Torchbooks, 1950.

Bakhtiar, Laleh. *Sufi.* London: Thames and Hudson, 1976.

Burckhardt, Titus. *Alchemy.* Translated by W. Stoddart. Baltimore: Penguin, 1971.

———. *Mystical Astrology According to Ibn 'Arabi.* Translated by Beshara Publications. Louisville, Ky.: Fons Vitae, 2001.

Eliade, Mircea. *History of Religious Ideas,* vol. 3. Translated by A. Hiltebeitel and D. Apostolos-Cappadona. Chicago: University of Chicago Press, 1985.

———. *Yoga: Immortality and Freedom.* Princeton: Princeton University Press, 1969.

Flowers, Stephen E. *Lords of the Left-Hand Path.* Rochester, Vt.: Inner Traditions, 2012.

Gilbhard, Hermann. *Die Thule Gesellschaft.* Munich: Kiessling, 1994.

Goodrick-Clarke, Nicholas. *The Occult Roots of Nazism.* Wellingborough, UK: Aquarian, 1985.

Jensen, Hans. *Sign, Symbol and Script.* Translated by George Unwin. New York: G. P. Putnam's Sons, 1969.

Kahn, Gabriel Mandel. *Arabic Script.* New York: Abbeville Press Publishers, 2000.

K'uan Yü, Lu. *Taoist Yoga: Alchemy and Immortality.* New York: Weiser, 1973.

Logan, Robert K. *The Alphabet Effect.* New York: William Morrow, 1986.

Rose, Detlev. *Die Thule Gesellschaft: Legende-Mythos-Wirklichkeit.* Tübingen: Grabert, 1994.

Sebottendorf(f), Rudolf von. *Bevor Hitler kam.* Munich: Deukula Verlag, 1933

———. *Die Praxis der alten türkischen Freimauerei: Der Schlüssel zum Verständnis der Alchemie.* Leipzig: Theosophisches Verlagshaus, 1924.

Shah, Idries. *The Sufis.* New York: Doubleday, 1964.

Wilhelm, Richard. *The Secret of the Golden Flower.* Translated by Cary F. Baynes. New York: Harcourt, Brace and Jovanovich, 1962.

Index